An Apology for the Life of
MAJOR GENERAL
GUNNING

An Apology for the Life of

MAJOR GENERAL

GUNNING

Containing

A full Explanation of the GUNNING MYSTERY,
and of the Author's Connexion with Mr. DUBERLEY's
FAMILY of SOHO-SQUARE

LATET ANGUIS IN HERBA.[1]

Edited and annotated by
GERRISH GRAY

Richmond
TIGER OF THE STRIPE
2012

First published in 1792
This annotated edition
first published in 2012 by
Tiger of the Stripe
50 Albert Road
Richmond
Surrey TW10 6DP
United Kingdom

© 2012 Gerrish Gray

ISBN 978-1-904799-49-8

Typeset in the UK by
Tiger of the Stripe

CONTENTS

PREFACE

THE text of this edition follows the original closely, although the punctuation and spelling have been sparingly modernised where they threatened to confuse the modern reader.

Footnotes, other than those in the Introduction, belong to the original *Apology* and are marked *, †, ¶, etc. Superscript numerals relate to my endnotes.

Names that are dashed out in the original are generally expanded but have occasionally been left unaltered to retain the flavour of artificial mystery fostered by the original edition in 1792.

The Introduction presents a brief background to the Gunning family and the unfortunate events which enveloped them. In particular, the so-called Gunning Mystery is re-examined: who was responsible for the allegedly forged correspondence between the General's daughter, Elizabeth, and the Duke of Marlborough's son, the Marquess of Blandford? Some surprising evidence, hidden in plain sight, has come to light. I hesitate to say that I have solved the Gunning Mystery but I have found evidence which, to my mind, points strongly to the forgeries being the work of someone whom I had previously assumed to be innocent.

Although much of the detail given in the *Apology* is corroborated by other sources, there are indications that it may itself be a forgery – or, perhaps, a hoax. The very fact that it presents General Gunning as a buffoon and scoundrel might, on its own, suggest that he is not the author, but this is not to say that it is in any way an inaccurate portrait. The *Apology*'s recycling of very old stories and anecdotes (some more than 200 years past their sell-by date) might equally suggest that it was written by a plodding hack or by the General himself, either desperate for a quick profit. There is one apparent reference to the republican Thomas Paine (p. 17), however, which must give the reader pause for thought about the *Apology*'s authenticity, even if the other preposterous claims about his progeny did not. Whether or not the *Apology* is the work of another hand (perhaps one of the many journalists covering the family's embarrassments), most of the details it contains of the Gunning Mystery and Duberley v. Gunning are correct.

GERRISH GRAY
Isleworth
August, 2012

INTRODUCTION

THE publication of this book in 1792 marked a low point for the Gunning family and for General Gunning in particular. Within five years, this supposed hero of Bunker Hill who claimed descent from Charlemagne and whose sisters had married into the highest levels of the aristocracy was to die in Naples, disgraced and apparently impoverished.

Major General John Gunning's *Apology* was published with the names of the main characters, Gunning (G———, G—nn—g), Duberley (D—ber—y), etc., obscured by the use of dashes. Since no-one at the time would have been unfamiliar with the two scandals surrounding the name of Gunning, the intention must not have been to protect the innocent or prevent the author from being sued for libel but to advertise the contents as being salacious. The title *Apology* seems to serve a similar purpose, for the author shows little remorse, and delights in recounting his many seductions. Despite the promise of the subtitle, the original edition leaves many questions about the so-called Gunning Mystery unanswered.

THE GUNNING FAMILY

The Gunnings were reasonably prosperous, if rather profligate, landed gentry with a family home at Castle Coote in Ireland, although it has been said that the family was originally from Cornwall.* The General's father, also John, was a barrister of the Middle Temple who had married Bridget (Biddy) Bourke, a daughter of Viscount Mayo, in 1731. Portraits show her to have

---

* Lady Conſtance Russell, *Three Generations of Fascinating Women*, 2nd edn, 1905, p. 95.

been very pretty and she was described as 'a young Lady of uncommon Accomplishment'.* The Honourable Bridget Bourke was not to be the Gunning family's last association with the aristocracy.

The newlyweds went to live at the old Manor House in Hemmingford Grey, Huntingdonshire, where their daughter Mary (usually called Maria) was born in 1732, Elizabeth in 1733, Catherine (Kitty) in 1735 andSophia in 1735. Their daughter Lissy was born in 1744. The date of John's birth is not recorded, but, as we shall see, the date 1742 given by the *Oxford Dictionary of National Biography*† seems to be at least a year out.

In 1740, presumably due to financial pressures, the family moved to Ireland, first to Roscommon and then to Dublin. Mrs Bellamy, the Irish actress, tells how, returning from the Dublin Theatre to Britain Street, she heard sounds of distress and came across 'a woman of most elegant figure, surrounded by four beautiful girls, and a sweet boy of about three years of age'. The distressed woman turned out to be Mrs Bridget Gunning whose possessions were being seized by the bailiffs.‡ The 'sweet boy', of course, was the future General. Since Mrs Bellamy makes it clear that this took place after Thomas Sheridan² took over the management of the theatre, it can have been no earlier than 1745, and John must have been about four (see below).

JOHN, ELIZABETH AND MARIA GUNNING

When they returned to England in the late 1740s, news of the beauty of the young John's sisters, Elizabeth and Maria, had preceded them. Despite their lack of dowries and their naïve

---

* *London Evening Post*, 28 October 1731.
† Given in the life of the General's daughter, Elizabeth.
‡ *An Apology for the Life of George Anne Bellamy,* 4th edn, vol. 1, 1786, p. 196–8.

ways, they soon attracted the attention of some of Britain's most eligible young men. Elizabeth met James Hamilton, sixth Duke of Hamilton on 16 January 1752 and they were married the following month, on St Valentine's day. In the March of that year, Maria married George Coventry, sixth Earl of Coventry whom she had first met in July 1750.

John was entered into Westminster School in 1751 and Maria and Elizabeth, visiting soon after, requested a holiday for the scholars, which was granted.* The school's records show that he was ten at the time of entering,[†] so must have been born in 1740 or 1741.

The Duke of Hamilton died in 1758 and in the following year Elizabeth married a handsome soldier called Jack Campbell. In 1770, her husband inherited the Dukedom of Argyll and Elizabeth's position in society was further enhanced. Such a rapid rise in the Gunning family's fortunes grabbed the public imagination; it was the stuff of fairy tales, or at least of the sentimental novels of the period and, many years later, it would have a bearing on the first scandal to engulf John Gunning and his family.

Despite the celebrity of his sisters, John Gunning seems to have lived in relative obscurity. He joined the army and, while a captain in the 49th Regiment of Foot, married Susannah Minifie, daughter of James Minifie DD, a somerset clergyman, in August 1768.[‡] Miss Minifie, like her sister Margaret, was a successful novelist, something which she was later to vehemently

---

* *Dublin Journal,* 29 June, 1751, quoted in *Three Generations,* p. 140.

† I am grateful to Rita Boswell, the School's Consultant Archivist, for this information.

‡ *St. James's Chronicle or the British Evening Post,* 6 August 1768 give 5 August. The DNB says 8 August but this was the date of the marriage allegation (a prerequisite of marriage by licence). It was presumably rather later in the month. Frank Frankfort Moore, 'The Plot of a Lady Novelist' in *A Georgian Pageant,* London: Hutchinson, 1908, has 1769 and, strangely, Lady Constance Russell says 1763.

Elizabeth Hamilton (*née* Gunning), Duchess of Hamilton,
later Duchess of Argyll. The Duke of Hamilton commissioned the painting from his
cousin, Gavin Hamilton, to celebrate his marriage to Elizabeth in 1752.

The young John Gunning.

deny, presumably to avoid the taint of commerce; since the shelves of every circulating library in England were groaning under the weight of prolix and gushing romantic novels bearing her maiden name upon their title pages, this achieved nothing but to undermine her credibility at a time when (as we shall see) it was sorely needed.

In early 1775, Gunning, now with the 43rd Foot, was appointed Deputy Adjutant General in North Britain with the rank of Lieutenant Colonel.* Not surprisingly, he was soon on American soil.

---

* *London Chronicle*, 14 February 1775.

Maria Coventry (*née* Gunning), Countess of Covenry, painted by Gavin Hamilton, probably in 1753.

Harold Murdock, an American amateur historian, has left us an imaginative reconstruction of Gunning's presence in Boston:[*]

> And now, as the darkness of an early spring day comes on, let us in imagination look into Earl Percy's dining-room and see what passes there. The newly lighted candles are burning brightly on the broad

[*] *Earl Percy's Dinner-Talk*, Boston: Houghton Mifflin, 1907, pp. 11–12.

table around which the Earl's eleven gueſts are sitting at their ease, all but three in the uniform of the royal army. The dinner is cleared away and the port and madeira are going the rounds. The Earl is chatting with a ſtrapping officer on his left whose handsome face is a fair legacy from the race of which he comes. This is Lieutenant-Colonel John Gunning of the 43d Foot, who has the honor to be the brother of the famous Gunning siſters, and through them a brother-in-law to the Duke of Argyll and to the Earl of Coventry. 'My siſter the Duchess,' and 'My siſter the late Countess of Coventry,' are well-worn phrases with Colonel Gunning, and within a year his pride has been ſtirred again by the marriage of his niece with Lord Stanley, the heir to the affluent Earl of Derby. The handsome Colonel speaks with something of a brogue, betraying his Irish origin, and if his memory is good he can recall dark days of childhood when the family fortunes were low, dishonor imminent, and when the situation was saved by warm-hearted George Anne Bellamy, of the Smock Alley Theatre in Dublin. But those days are long paſt, and Colonel Gunning glories not only in his connection with great families in England, and in his rapid rise in the army, but also in an honeſt and complacent conviction that he is thirty-second in descent from Charlemagne.

In General Orders, 19 June 1775 we find:

> The Commander-in-chief returns his moſt grateful thanks to Major-general Howe for the extraordinary exertion of his military abilities on the 17th inſtant. He returns his thanks also to Major-general Clinton and Brigadier Pigot for the share they took in the success of the day, as well as to Lieutenant-colonels Nesbitt, Abercromby, Gunning, and Clarke, Majors Butler, Williams, Bruce, Tupper, Spenlove, Small, and Mitchel, and the reſt of the officers and soldiers, who by remarkable efforts of courage and gallantry overcame every disadvantage, and drove the rebels from the redoubt and ſtrongholds on the heights of Charlestown, and gained a complete victory.*

By this time he was serving with the 82nd Foot. In truth, Gunning's military career has left few traces and was probably

---

*   Paul Harris Nicolas, *Hiſtorical Record of the Royal Marine Forces,* London: Thomas and William Boone, 1845, vol. 1, p. 87

very undistinguished. In November 1779 we find him presiding over the court martial of one Garret Bush in New York:[*]

[Extract of the General Court Martial whereof Lieut. Colonel John GUNNING was President, held at New York between 16 November 1779 and 24 November 1779.]

Friday the 19th November 1779.
The Court met pursuant to Adjournment.
Garret BUSH Inhabitant of Staten Island, was brought Prisoner before the Court, and accused of Aiding and acting as a Guide to the Rebels on Staten Island in taking a part of His Majesty's Light Dragoons.

Captain COGLE of the 1st Battalion of New Jersey Volunteers being duly Sworn deposed that one James BARTLEY came to him at his Post at Decker's Ferry on Staten Island, and informed him that the person who guided the Rebels on a certain Night wore a Snuff coloured pair of Velvet Breeches, a sort of Callicoe cross barr'd Jacket with Linnen backs to it, a little round Hat bound with Velvet, and a Ribband buckled round the Crown, that the said James BARTLEY came from the Rebel Shore, and informed him of the above, that he (the Witness) then went and pursued him; that he went into several Houses, but could find nothing like the described Cloaths, that at last he went to the House the prisoner formerly lived at, and there found the prisoner with a Hat on his Head exactly answering BARTLEY'S description; that as soon as BARTLEY saw the Prisoner he cried out 'that is the man.'
    Q: (by the Court) – How long a time was there between the Light Dragoons having been attempted to be carried off to the time the man gave you the information of the Prisoner?
    A. About Six Weeks.
    Q: Did you say that the people in whose House the Cloaths were found, said they belonged to the Prisoner?
    A: Yes.

---

[*]   UK National Archives, WO 71, vol. 91, pp. 19–22.

James BARTLEY Soldier in the 1st Battalion New Jersey Volunteers, being duly Sworn deposed that about three months ago or something more, he was with the Rebels when they crossed over at the burnt Island, that he believes the intention of the Rebels was to take some Light Horse, but finding that the Party at Decker's Ferry was too Strong for them, they only lay in wait upon the road to take a patrole as it should pass; that two Light Horsemen were passing by the Place where they lay, and the rebels fired upon them: that while they were firing, a Guide who belonged to the Rebels, ran to a House hard by and brought the Prisoner to the Gate, and asked him if he were willing to go with them to guide them back to their Boat, and he said he was, but that they must make haste, for that if he should be found out, he would be hung – that the Prisoner then did guide them to the Marsh, when they let him go as they then knew the road very well.

Q: (by the Court) – Do you know of your own knowledge, that the Prisoner went with his own accord or was he forced?

A: He went of his own accord.

The Court Adjourned for further Evidence.

Monday 22nd November 1779.
The Court met pursuant to Adjournment not having further Evidence the Prisoner was put upon his Defence.

The Prisoner Garret BUSH being put upon his Defence, declared to the Court, that on a Sunday Evening he was going home, when the rebels took him just as he came out of the door and forced him to guide them to their Boat; that as soon as he got to the Marsh, they let him go.

The Prisoner called upon Mr. Benjamin PARKER Inhabitant of the City of New York who being duly sworn deposed that he has known the Prisoner five Years that he enlisted as a Waggoner under Colonel SHERRIFFE: that he never knew him at all to be suspected as an Enemy to British Government, and has always understood that he has done his Duty very well upon Staten Island.

He further called upon Mr. Isaac DECKER Inhabitant of Staten Island who being duly Sworn deposed that he has known the Prisoner from a Child that he always looked upon him as a friend to British Government, and he never heard that his Character was the least Suspected by any one.

The Court having duly considered the Evidence for and againſt
BUSH, together with what he had to offer in his Defence, is of Opinion That he aċted as a Guide to the Rebels in breach of the nineteenth
Article of the fourteenth Seċtion of the Articles of War; but that it was
by Compulsion and it doth therefore Acquit him.

John BLUCKE   J: GUNNING
Assiſtant Deputy Judge Advocate   Lt. Col. President

Confirmed
H. CLINTON

If Gunning's own account is to be believed, he was probably
too busy practising the arts of seduction to play any very important part in the hostilities (p. 17 ff.). The British army, which
Gunning credits with teaching him the 'more refined mysteries
of the debauchee' (p. 4) seems to have been so preoccupied
with such activities that it is remarkable that the Revolutionary
War dragged on until 1783.

DOMESTIC BLISS

What attracted John Gunning to Susannah Minifie is something of a mystery. Perhaps she was pretty in her youth, although the pictures of her in later life do nothing to support this
idea. She certainly did not represent an advantageous match on
the scale of Maria's and Elizabeth's marriages. As the daughter
of a country parson, she would not have brought John any social advantage and is unlikely to have brought much of a dowry
either. Susannah seems to have been quite well educated but,
like her husband, no great intellectual. As her *Letter** amply

---

* *A letter from Mrs. Gunning addressed to His Grace the Duke of Argyll,* London :
Printed for the author, 1791. I have relied on the Dublin reprint of the same year for
quotations.

demonstrates, she was severely afflicted by verbal incontinence. Unlikable though Gunning is, it is hard not to feel a twinge of sympathy for anyone exposed to such a 'cataract of eloquence,' to use the General's own words (p. 39).

Before their marriage, Susannah had written two novels with her sister Margaret, *The Histories of Lady Francis S——, and Lady Caroline S——* (1763)* and *The Picture* (1766).† *Barford Abbey* (1768)‡ and *The Count de Poland* (1780) which were formerly attributed to Susannah are now said by some to be by her sister Margaret§ and it may be that she only resumed her literary career after her estrangement from the General.

THE YOUNGER ELIZABETH GUNNING

In 1769 John and Susannah's only child, Elizabeth, was born. As the niece of the famous Gunning sisters and daughter of a romantic novelist, she seemed destined to be the heroine of her own romance and it is unlikely that her foolish mother or her self-centred and libidinous father did anything to rein in her fantasies.

Much of her childhood was spent with the family of her aunt, the Duchess of Argyll, and she must surely have expected

---

* Four volumes, nearly 1,000 pages (albeit in duodecimo with only about 135 words per page). The very long subscription list (over 900 copies) is impressive and may provide a clue to Susannah's attraction. The sisters must have made a very healthy profit from the publication of their first novel.

† A mere three volumes and about 700 pages. Like the first book, the title proclaims that it is 'by the Miss Minifies, of Fairwater in Somersetshire'. I have seen no evidence to substantiate the claim that it is the work of Margaret alone.

‡ A novel whose love interest is a Lord Darcy, sadly a very bland creation compared to Jane Austen's Mr Darcy.

§ Viginia Blain, Patricia Clements and Isobel Grundy, *The Feminist Companion to Literature in English,* London: Batsford, 1990. This is stated without supporting evidence or references, so the claim is impossible to assess.

that her own charms would one day win her a place in the aristocracy. There was, according to some commentators, a major problem, in that, talented and charming as she might have been, she was rather plain and, much as many might wish it to be otherwise, men do tend to favour pretty girls over plain ones. Frank Moore, without quoting sources says:

> The result of the union was a daughter of considerable plainness, and people said that in this respect she resembled her mother's rather than her father's family. It seems that while the Gunning tradition was beauty, the Minifie tradition was a nose, and it soon became apparent that it was impossible to combine the two with any satisfactory artisitic results. The young lady had made an honest attempt to do so, but her failure was emphatic. She had eyes that suggested in a far-off way the long-lashed orbs of her aunts, but that unlucky Minifie nose was so prominent a feature that it caused the attention of even the most indulgent critic to be riveted upon it, to the exclusion of the rest of her face. The charitably-disposed among her friends affirmed that she would be passably good-looking if it were not for her nose; the others said that she would be positively plain if it were not for her eyes.[*]

While this may be true, Moore is clearly striving for effect and proves his unreliability by referring to the wretched girl throughout as Catherine.[†] Another, generally more reliable commentator, Lady Constance Russell, also insists that Elizabeth was 'neither handsome nor clever,' adding in a footnote that 'all the prints of her make her decidedly very plain'.[‡] Elizabeth's cousin, Lady Charlotte Campbell called her ugly.[§]

Others seem to have considered the young Elizabeth both good-looking and clever. The stipple engraving by Bartolozzi

[*] *Georgian Pageant*, pp. 148–9.
[†] There was a Catherine or Kitty Gunning, sister to the more famous Maria and Elizabeth, but More's story clearly relates to Elizabeth.
[‡] *Three Generations*, p. 136.
[§] Quoted in *Three Generations*, p. 136.

after a painting by Saunders (p. xxiii) is pretty enough, while the engraving by Mackenzie after a painting by Sir Robert Ker Porter makes her look a little bovine but then the execution itself is rather crude, and the print by Gillray (not known for his flattery) of her straddling a cannon (p. xxix) is both saucy and attractive (if one favours women draped across gun barrels) – but had Gillray ever seen his subject? In another Gillray print (p. xli), she is too swaddled in bedclothes for any sensible judgement of her looks to be made. However, the *Gentleman's Magazine* refers to

> General Gunning, whose beautiful daughter is in possession of those graces for which her aunts, the late Duchess of Argyle and Lady Coventry, were so justly famed.[*]

One anonymous commentator referred to her as a young lady who possessed 'much ornamental and substantial excellence'. Elizabeth's novels may seem a little silly to the modern reader, but they are not badly constructed and they show every sign of being written by by a well-educated person. Her translation of Bernard de Fontenelle's *Conversations on the Plurality of Worlds*[†] captures the charm and wit of the original, indicating a lively intelligence and sense of humour. There are, it is true, some strange quirks of this translation, not least that Parisians are referred to throughout as Persians. Since there are other obvious mistakes which have survived from the first edition to the second, it seems likely that these are printer's errors which Elizabeth has failed to pick up. Perhaps, like many authors, she had a profound dislike of re-reading her work in proof.

To us it only matters whether she was plain or pretty, stupid or clever, in so far as this may aid our interpretation of the so-

---

[*] 1791, vol. 1, p. 229.
[†] Also published by Tiger of the Stripe.

called Gunning Mystery, that scandal which was to have such a profound effect on her father, her mother and herself.

THE GUNNING MYSTERY

> The Gunnings are still playing the fool, and perhaps someone with them...[*]

The General himself referred to it as a mystery and, although he claims on the title page of his *Apology* to offer a full explanation, his story – putting most of the blame on his wife and the rest on his daughter – is not entirely convincing. More than two hundred years after the event, it is still a mystery. Mrs Gunning's *Letter*, crammed into ninety-eight close-packed pages, does much to elucidate her character but nothing to explain the mystery. Elizabeth protested her innocence under oath at the time (p. 59) but said very little about the matter in later life. Someone is lying – perhaps everyone (at least in the Gunning household) is lying.

The trouble seems to have started on the death of Elizabeth's aunt Elizabeth, the Duchess of Argyll, in 1790. The young Elizabeth, this clever/stupid, pretty/plain woman of twenty-one, brought up on romantic novels and more romantic tales of her beautiful aunts, had been staying with the Duchess. Given her upbringing, it was unsurprising that she had formed a romantic attachment to her cousin George, the Marquess of Lorne. It may never have occurred to her that a marriage between her and George would not be considered a good match by his family. George's sister Charlotte[†] may have expressed the family's attitude, albeit with considerable spite:

---

[*]   Horace Walpole, letter to Miss Berry, 22 Jan. 1791, in *Letters*, vol. vi, p. 384.

[†]   Lady Charlotte Bury (née Campbell), a popular novelist whose *Flirtation* (1827), though of doubtful merit, was a great success.

Engraving by Francesco Bartolozzi of Elizabeth Gunning after a painting by Saunders.
Reproduced by kind permission of New York Public Library.

My brother, in the first éclat of youth, novelty, and good looks, had little leisure or inclination to think of an ugly cousin at home, but that unfortunate girl chose to imagine otherwise.*

* Quoted in *Three Generations,* p. 136.

On the death of her aunt, Elizabeth left the grieving family and returned to her parents in St James's Place, but it appears that she did not abandon her hopes of an alliance with her cousin. Despite what Charlotte says, is it likely that Elizabeth (and the press) would have imagined interest on George's side if none had existed?

Even before the Duchess's death, rumours had started circulating, some linking Elizabeth with George, others with the Duke of Marlborough's son, the Marquess of Blandford:

> Miss Gunning will soon be a Marchioness. She has *shot* the Marquess of Blandford through his heart, and she is to wear it as a *trophy*.[*]

Afterwards, it was suggested by the General and others that Elizabeth, perhaps at the prompting of her mother, had invented a romance with Blandford to rekindle Lorne's waning ardour. This rather implies that, contrary to Charlotte Bury's assertion, there had been some ardour to wane.

To have pretended to some non-existent attachment would not, perhaps, have been the most heinous crime that a young lady might commit, even supposing that we believe Elizabeth to be guilty. Unfortunately, a number of forged letters surfaced which purported to prove Blandford's intentions towards her and again the suspicion fell upon Elizabeth or her mother. Who, after all, could more skilfully concoct such things than a romantic novelist? To the delight of newspaper proprietors, this soon turned into a full-blown scandal.

THE FORGED LETTERS

The story of the forged letter or letters broke in early 1791. One newspaper summarised the matter thus:

---

[*]   *Gazetteer and New Daily Advertiser,* 7 August 1790

About two years ago, the Marquis of Blandford met the accomplished Miss Gunning at a Ball, and had the good fortune to engage the lady's hand as his partner for the evening. Soon after, Miss Gunning received a letter from the Marquis, as she believed, expressing very tender sentiments of admiration, and soliciting permission to visit and correspond with her. The rank and pretensions of the Marquis were indisputable recommendations of his suit; and a correspondence was begun, which General Gunning was not indisposed to countenance, as he was informed that the Duke of Marlborough was perfectly acquainted with his son's attachment. The correspondence went on for some months, until the Duke of Argyle suggested some doubts of the Duke of Marlborough's being acquainted with the affair.

General Gunning wrote a letter to the Noble Duke, communicating the penchant of the Marquis, and saying, that unless it was with his Grace's perfect consent, he would not suffer the correspondence to go on. That this letter might be conveyed with becoming attention, the General despatched his own servant with it to Woodstock; and after a proper interval, he received, by the same messenger, an answer from the Duke, assuring the General of his perfect respect for the young lady, to whose merits he was no stranger; and that an alliance with the ancient family of the General would be highly desirable to every branch of his House.*

A less pompous or slightly more intelligent man than the General might have wondered why the Duke of Marlborough would consider an alliance with the Gunning family 'highly desirable.' However, the General, who boasted of his family's (extremely doubtful) descent from the Emperor Charlemagne,[†] clearly considered the English Duke and Prince of the Holy Roman Empire something of a *parvenu*. When shown the Duke of Marlborough's purported letter, his brother, Lord Charles

---

*   *Lloyds Evening Post*, 21 February 1791.

†   Writing to the *Public Advertiser* about his sister Elizabeth on 24 December 1790, General Gunning said, 'she was certainly of illustrious descent, who derived her birth in the thirty-third generation from CHARLEMAGNE.' It is possible, but not perhaps probable, as Gunning later claimed, that this letter is a forgery.

George Campbell, Marquess of Lorne, by Henry Edridge.

Spencer, denounced it as a crude forgery. The seal was said to be either a copy or an old version, no longer used.

Elizabeth and her mother denied any part in the forgery but the messenger, Gunning's groom, said that rather than deliver the General's letter to the Duke at Blenheim Palace, he had gone no further than Salt Hill,[*] thus implicating Elizabeth and Susannah in this deception. It is said that the General,

> shocked with this information, queſtioned Mrs. and Miss Gunning; told them that a forgery had been praĉtised either *by* or *on* them; and with the authority of a husband and a father demanded the truth. He received no other answer, than that they were equally dupes of the fraud, if it was a fraud.[†]

---

[*] Near Slough, on the way from London to Blenheim, but less than a third of the way there.

[†] *Lloyds Evening Poſt*, 21 February 1791.

Gunning's response was what one would expect from an officer and a gentleman – or at least, *this* officer. He gave his wife and daughter twenty-four hours to justify their conduct. If they failed to do so, they must leave his house forever. In his *Apology*, the General claims that the ladies' expulsion had been agreed by a 'Grand Council' of the family to protect *his* reputation (p. 52). However, there is nothing in Mrs Gunning's *Letter* which hints that they were party to this, nor in Elizabeth's indignant letter to her father:*

Monday Evening.

TURN'D from your doors defenceless pennyless and robb'd by you of what is and ever will be dearer than my life—my character—Stigmatized for forgeries which those who really did forge the letters and *you* Sir *muſt* know I am as innocent of as heaven is free from fraud you who I never in my life offended in thought word or deed to caſt me out upon the wide world as a guilty creature when you know my heart would not have harboured a thought, that could have dishonoured you, myself or my sex; and after you had thrown me off to pursue me as you would the bittereſt of enemies, to raise up false witnesses to crush that child whom you should have proteƈted with your life; innocent I again repeat you *know* me to be, even had I been guilty, which God be praised I am not, ſtill *you* should have screened me, and your chaſtisements should have been softened by pity; you call me unfortunate, I am unfortunate; who has made me so? This unfortunate will never appear in your presence, 'till you announce, and that in the moſt publick and moſt unequivocal manner, to the whole world, how much she has been wronged by scandalous contrivances and unheard of calumny.

(Signed)   E. GUNNING.

---

*   Quoted in Susannah Gunning's *Letter*, pp. 94–5. It is almoſt worthy of one of Mrs Gunning's overblown novels, though Elizabeth's writing is as deficient in commas as her mother's is superabundant in italics. Written after Elizabeth's expulsion from the family home, it is sometimes referred to as her final letter to her father, but, as we shall see (p. xlii), she may have written to him shortly before his death.

Elizabeth as Suspect

Mother and daughter were given refuge by Blandford's aunt, the dowager Duchess of Bedford, in Pall Mall and, from the beginning, popular opinion was mostly on their side, although *The Times* remarked rather sourly that

> Miss Gunning, though handsome, is not so much celebrated for her beauty, as for her accomplished manners and amiable disposition. – It is therefore, with great regret, we observe, that vanity should have so far triumphed over discretion, as to have given rise to the many remarks which naturally occur on a late transaction.[*]

Horace Walpole clearly believed that Elizabeth (whom he called Gunnilda), her mother and her aunt Margaret were in league:

> Here is a shocking, not a fatal, codicil to Gunnilda's Story. But first I should tell you, that two days after the explosion, the Signora Madre took a postchaise to Blenheim; but, not finding the Duke and Duchess there, she inquired where the Marquis was, and pursued him to Sir Henry Dashwood's: finding him there, she began about her poor daughter; but he interrupted her, said there was an end put to all that, and desired to lead her to her chaise, which he insisted on doing, and did. I think this another symptom of the Minifry being accomplices to the daughter's enterprise.[†]

Elsewhere, the accusations against Elizabeth were given little credence:

> Such is the vague story, and which we have willingly submitted to relate, absurd as it is, because the ladies are not unwilling that the gross fiction which has produced such serious consequences to them should go forth; its own improbability being its refutation. Here is a stratagem

---

[*]   23 February 1791
[†]   To Agnes Berry, 18 Feb. 1791, *Letters*, vol. vi, p. 399.

Elizabeth Gunning saucily draped over a cannon in a detail from Gillray's *The Seige [sic] of Blenheim – or a new system of Gunning, discoverd* (see full cartoon, p. xxx), published 5 March 1791. It is a print replete with military terms and sexual innuendo.

The Seige of Blenheim. Elizabeth is draped on the cannon firing forged letters at Blenheim Palace but fire is being returned, presumably by the Duke, who (not to put too fine a point on it) is shitting on them from afar. The General sneaks off saying, 'I find our Stratagem won't take effect, & therefore I'll be off; & manoeuvre; – any common Soldier can lead *on*, to any attack, but it takes the skill of a *General* to bring off his forces with honor after a defeat –'. Meanwhile, Elizabeth is crying. 'O Mother! Mother! my masked Battery is discovered, & we shall be blown up! – O, Mother, Mother, we must raise the Siege immediately, & take refuge under the Duchess's cover'd way, & there act on the defensive: O Mother, Mother! it's all your fault, say what you will!'

Mrs Gunning replies, 'Good Heav'ns! who could have thought that the Seige of a Coronet would have ended in smoke and stink! – well I'll take my *Affidavit* that I know nothing at all about the matter.'

Blandford's aunt, the ageing Duchess of Bedford, lifts up her hooped skirt, saying, 'Come under my Protection, deary's [sic]! I'll hide you in Bedfordshire; & find you one of my Granny-boys, to play with Missy.'

without a motive, and a forgery working to no benefit. The Marquis of Blandford could not be drawn into a marriage by a correspondence of which he was ignorant; and it is surely not a very likely means for the young Lady to engage the heart of any other Nobleman (for that has been suggested), by pretending to be violently enamoured herself to the Marquis – her letters are made to breathe the warmest and most tender affection for him.

The fact is, that deep, dark and mysterious as the plot has been, it will turn out to be an artful machination in a quarter from which the young lady should rather have received protection than injury; practised for the purpose of drawing off the affections of a young Nobleman really enamoured of her charms, and to whose passion they were adverse.

Miss Gunning was, equally with her mother, the dupe of the contrivance; and unless gallantry shall rouse Gentlemen to inquire, before they decide, she may become the victim!*

A wag in the *Morning Daily Advertiser*† wrote:

It is thought in fashionable circles, that Miss GUNNING has really been imposed upon, and that the heir of BLENHEIM has not written the mysterious letters, as the *spelling* is good and the *grammar* not amiss!

As well as the lack of a convincing motive, there are other reasons for doubting Elizabeth's guilt. Mrs Gunning argued in her *Letter*,‡ that Elizabeth would never have written 'St. James Place' for 'St. James's Place'. An anonymous commentator doubted the significance of this§ but the habitués of *St. James's* would not be seen dead in *St. James*. Mrs Gunning quotes a letter purporting to be from Elizabeth to Mrs Bowen:¶

Tuesday

Dear Mrs. Bowen.

As you seem to be in the confidence of Mama, I think it right I tell you that you may hint to her that my affections are engaged to my C———n L——d L———— and I am not to be married to L——d B———————— as she seems to think; will you be so good as to get the enclosed copied for me?

Affectionately yours,
(Signed) E. Gunning

* *Lloyd's Evening Post*, 21 February, 1791.
† 26 February 1791.
‡ *Letter*, p. 57.
§ *Narrative*, p. 11.
¶ *Letter*, p. 50.

Mrs Gunning states:*

> There is this *little* omission in the spelling the *first* name only one *small* letter more than the name requires to be spelt with, which must have been particularly *negligent* in my daughter to have *added,* as she *certainly* has written the name *too* often for *ignorance* to have afforded *her* any shelter.

Confusingly, the *omission* referred to by Mrs Gunning seems to be the *addition* ('one *small* letter more') of the letter *e* in Lorne. Since almost everyone except Mrs Gunning herself spelt the name *with* the *e*, this is hardly compelling evidence.

The letter which Mrs Bowen said Elizabeth had enclosed was, according to Mrs Gunning, written on a half sheet of paper, without date or direction and read as follows:†

> Sir,
>
> I must say I wish you and your daughter had known your own minds in respect of my son.
>
>   I am your most
>   obedient
>   Signed at length ——————————
>   but the name mis-spelt.

None of this makes much sense. One minute Elizabeth is supposed to be forging a letter from the Duke of Marlborough welcoming a match between Elizabeth and his son, the next she is forging a letter from him regretting her decision not to marry him – all this to ensnare her cousin, the Marquess of Lorne.

Elizabeth swore her innocence in an affidavit on 14 February (Appendix, p. 59), which the waspish Horace Walpole dismissed out of hand:‡

---

* *Letter,* p. 51.
† *Letter,* p. 51.
‡ To Agnes Berry, 18 Feb. 1791, *Letters,* vol. vi, pp. 399–400.

… the next day, taking two of the Duchess of Bedford's servants for witnesses, she went before a justice of peace, swore to her innocence and ignorance throughout, even of the note to Mrs. Bowen; and then said to the magistrate, 'Sir, from my youth you may imagine I do not know the solemnity of an oath; but, to convince you I do, I know my salvation depends on what I have now sworn.' Solve all this, if you can! Is it madness? Does even romance extend its inventions so far? or its dispensations?

As we shall see later (p. xliv), it is possible that Walpole was right to doubt Elizabeth's innocence.

SUSANNAH AS SUSPECT

Mrs Gunning, it must be said, was not only a liar but a very brazen and foolish one. In her *Letter* she says:

Why have the *combined plotters*, for none but the *tools* of mischief would have so *meanly* employed themselves, amongst their other *ridiculous insertions*, in the *news-papers* accused me of Novel writing; *particularly* a book called Waltham-Abbey; which is made up *they say* of *tricks*, of *stratagem*, and of *forged letters*. I must *assure* them *their* mistake is a *very* palpable one, for though to have been the author of *that* book might possibly have done honour to my *genius;* yet, as I *never* have seen such a book written, I *cannot* without great *injustice*, and *greater* presumption, lay any *claim* to the *credit* of being its *writer*.[*]

There never was a novel called *Waltham Abbey*[†] (which is a well-known town north of London). There is, however, *Barford Abbey* (1768), an epistolary novel traditionally ascribed to Susannah. Even if this book was actually by her sister, Margaret Minife, it is preposterous for Mrs Gunning to deny all knowledge of it, especially, as her *Letter* makes clear that Margaret

---

[*]   *Letter*, p. 59. The breathless style and over-fondness for italics are typical of the Minifie sisters' novels.

[†]   As an exhaustive search of the Library of Congress, COPAC and other catalogues confirms.

was staying with the Gunnings at the time that the scandal broke.* To change the name to *Waltham Abbey* was disingenuous.† To claim that she was no novelist when *The Histories of Lady Francis S——, and Lady Caroline S——* credits the Minifie sisters on its title page is quite absurd. It is hard to avoid the conclusion that Mrs Gunning was in the habit of lying. However, the orthographical objections to Elizabeth's authorship of the letter purporting to be from Marlborough presumably apply to Susannah as well; she would hardly have introduced what she considered spelling mistakes into any forgeries she intended to deceive. If Mrs Gunning *had* forged the letter(s), what would she have hoped to gain from it? General Gunning was temporarily placated, but she must surely have expected that the forgery would soon be detected. On the other hand, she could hardly have expected to get away with her denial of being a novelist either, so Mrs Gunning remains a possible, although unlikely, suspect.

The General as Suspect

If, for the moment, we exclude the mother and daughter from the list of suspects, who is left? The 'quarter from which the young lady should rather have received protection than injury' referred to by the author of the *Reynold's Evening Post* article is surely Gunning himself. Mrs Gunning points the finger of blame at the General through the agency of the groom and two others, Captain and Mrs Essex Bowen. Unfortunately, unless one believes that Gunning took a sadistic pleasure in humiliating his daughter, he seems to have had no motive.

---

* *Letter,* p. 31.

† It was also particularly pointless. *Barford Abbey* contains no plot or subplot concerning forged letters. Of course, the novel itself consists of fictitious letters but there is a clear distinction between fiction and fraud.

Gillray's *Betty Canning reviv'd – A peep at the Conjuration of Mary Squires and the Gispey Family*, published 25 March 1791, is another reference to the Gunning Mystery. In 1753, Canning, an eighteen-year-old maid, claimed to have been abducted and held prisoner by one Mother Wells and a Gypsy called Mary Squires. Henry Fielding, in his role as a magistrate, was taken in by Canning's perjured testimony.

In the doorway, the Gunnings' groom stands in front of a signpost to Blenheim, saying, 'I'm ready to ride, or swear, or any thing.' Betty Canning (Elizabeth Gunning) is saying to Mother Wells (General Gunning), 'I *Swear*, that I never wish'd or tried directly or indirectly to get a Coronet; that I never saw or writ to Lord B– or Lord L–, in all my Life; – that men are my aversion; – & that I never had any thing to do with, with [sic] the Groom, in all my born days; – will that do, Dad?' She kisses not a Bible but a pack of playing cards.

While the Devil under the table melts his sealing wax, the General replies, 'Well done, Bett! We'll get through the Business I'll warrant you; – we can write all sorts of hands, we've got all kinds of Seals, & with the assistance of our old Friend under the Table we shall be able to gull them yet daughter but I must be Mum.'

Behind Elizabeth, her mother is saying, 'That's right, my sweet innocent Angel! say Grace boldly! make haste my dear lovely Lambkin! – I'll soon blow up the Fire, while Nawntee Peg helps to cook up the Coronets; we'll get you a nice tit bit for Dinner before we're done, my dear little deary.'

'Puff away Sister.' says Margaret Minifie, 'the Soup will soon boil – law's me, how soft the Green Peas do grow, & how they Jump about in the Pot when you Puff your Bellows!' Behind her is a copy of '*Waltham Abbey*' by Peg Niffy.'

Picture courtesy of the Lewis Walpole Library, Yale University.

The Sinister Captain Bowen

We can surely disregard the groom as a principal. He would have neither the motive nor the capacity to perpetrate such a scheme on his own. However, the sinister and shadowy figure of Captain Bowen makes a tempting suspect. A relation by marriage of the General's, Bowen seduced the unfortunate Mary Anne Talbot and had her dress in men's clothing. She accompanied Bowen as his foot-boy under the name John Taylor. Bowen was killed and Talbot wounded at the battle for Valenciennes in May 1793. Still disguised as a man, she served in the Royal Navy for several years.

Certainly Mrs Gunning suspected Captain Bowen, and his wife, in the conspiracy.

How Many Forgeries?

At this point, however, we must remember that there are a number of possible forgery scenarios: the several letters from Blandford and the one from Marlborough may have been forgeries or only the one from Marlborough was. There were also other letters which seem to show Elizabeth's guilt, but which, according to Mrs Gunning, are further forgeries perpetrated by the Bowens, so there may be one forgery by one forger, several forgeries by one forger or even several forgeries by several forgers.* It is also certain that a great many lies have been told. If Elizabeth and her mother wee telling the truth, it would seem that the Bowens and the groom were lying, and *vice versa*. If Mrs Gunning was telling the truth (and her blatant lie about being a novelist does not inspire confidence), the Bowens also forged letters purporting to be by Elizabeth.

---

* Were this an Agatha Christie novel, it would probably transpire that one forgery had been created by several different people. Fortunately, it is not.

BLANDFORD OR MARLBOROUGH AS SUSPECTS

If we accept for one moment that the original correspondence between Blandford and Elizabeth might have been genuine,[*] the obvious suspects for forging the Marlborough letter are Elizabeth and/or Blandford. Asked by the General whether the match had Marlborough's approval, either of them might be tempted to concoct the evidence until Blandford had managed to convince his father to acquiesce. Alternatively (and far more probably, since there could be little likelihood that Marlborough would contemplate such a union), Blandford might have assured Elizabeth of his father's approval and then been obliged to furnish the evidence. This was the suspicion expressed in the *Attic Miscellany*:[†]

> A person, unacquainted with the parties, uninfluenced by prejudice, and guided only by the dictates of reason, would naturally have fixed his suspicions on a *gentleman,* who, fearing disapprobation where he wished for concurrence, *might* have had recourse to a deception in order to ensure the continuation of an intercourse that was flattering to his mind, in the hope that time's efficient hand might remove obstacles which, for the present, appeared insurmountable.

However, while it is possible to believe that Blandford might have bribed Gunning's groom to deliver the forgery, it is hard to believe that he would have bribed the groom and both the Bowens to implicate the woman he supposedly loved. Either Elizabeth was guilty or someone had a good reason to discredit her.

While Blandford's father, the fourth Duke of Marlborough, might well have disapproved of any liaison between his son and Elizabeth Gunning and would certainly have had the means to suborn witnesses and discredit her, it is hard to believe that he

[*] The contemporary press seemed quite ready to believe that both Lorne and Blandford were smitten with Elizabeth.
[†] Vol. 2, issue 19, 1790, p. 237.,

xxxviii   *Introduction*

would have bothered to do so. He could simply have forbidden an alliance between Blandford and Elizabeth.

CRIMINAL CONVERSATION

Even after the deaths of Gunning's sisters, the Countess of Coventry and the Duchess of Argyll, their noble families may have been perceived to stand guarantors of the General's debts; and the prospect of an advantageous marriage for Elizabeth must have enhanced his creditworthiness. With the breaking scandal of the forged Blandford letters, he was suddenly seen to be a very poor risk. The creditors circled and Gunning soon found himself in the debtors' prison.

Why James Duberley, the clothier who supplied the uniforms for the 65th Regiment of Foot, should pay Gunning's debts is uncertain. It is possible that the two had a mutually beneficial relationship. As the American scientist and entrepreneur Benjamin Thompson (later Count Rumford) discovered, the supply of uniforms to the British army could be a very profitable enterprise. On the other hand, Duberley may have been motivated by no other consideration than friendship. Whatever his motive, Duberley was soon to regret his kindness.

On 25 September 1791, Gunning slept at the clothier's house in East Sheen. The next morning, Gunning left for London. Duberley also went to London in search of a horse for his intended journey to Bath. He sent the horse to Sheen with a request that his wife should take care of it until he left London and was surprised when his servant returned and informed him that his wife had herself left for London on the Mortlake stage coach.* When he managed to find her after two days, she told

---

* Anon, *Trial between James Duberley and Major-General Gunning*, London: Ridgway, 1792, p.6.

him that their mutual friend Mrs Gardiner had persuaded her to go to the theatre in Richmond. In reality, she had been in the company of General Gunning.

Duberley's case for criminal conversation against Gunning commenced at the Court of King's Bench on Wednesday 22 February 1792. Duberley's counsel, Mr Erskine, demanding damages of £10,000, gave a most powerful address to the jurors, part of which is said to have drawn tears from many hearers. He described the General as old and infirm and much crippled with gout.* Surprisingly, since we know that he was no more than fifty-two, Gunning's own clerk, John Rogers, said that the General 'appeared to be about sixty, and was very infirm with gout,'† and his defence counsel, Edward Bearcroft KC, described Gunning as 'a mummy'.‡ At the time of the trial Mrs Duberley was not yet twenty-six (see p. xli f.n.), half the General's age.

Gunning's defence relied partly on the suggestion that Duberley was in some way complicit in his wife's adultery, a defence which had restricted damages to £10 in the famous Cibber v. Sloper case of 1738. He also relied on the assertion that Duberley himself kept a Mrs Kippa, a woman 'of easy access' and continued to visit her after his marriage. It was also claimed that he had been seen sitting on the lap of Mrs Gardiner, 'wife of a gentleman of rank resident in Paris',§ while the General sat on Mrs Duberley's lap.

Bearcroft hinted at some very indecorous behaviour in the Duberley household:

---

*   *Walker's Hibernian Magazine*, Feb. 1792, p. 161.

†   *The Diary or Woodfall's Register*, 23 Feb. 1792.

‡   *Town and Country Magazine*, Feb. 1792, p. 54.

§   Variously Gardner, Gardener, Gardiner and either of Paris or Brussells. Mrs Gardiner carefully absented herself from the country for the duration of the trial.

He could not tell all the games they played at; but one of them was blindman's bluff. The old, lame and crazy child of sixty,* playing with the reſt, with Mrs. Gardiner, and Mr. and Mrs. Duberley, when the candles were put out, sometimes tumbled down; and when the servant went up ſtairs she found the carpet in a ſtrange situation; indeed, it was all rolled, and rumpled, and powdered, and the ladies [sic] heads all un-powdered, and their hair very much dishevelled and one of Mrs. Gardiner's gold ear-ring [sic] was found upon the carpet.[†]

This approach seemed to work for the defendant, as the trial judge, Lord Kenyon, while describing Gunning as 'an hoary, abominable, degraded creature', suggested that Duberley was not entitled to large damages,

> as it appeared he had connived at several unwarranted levities in his own house, and had visited a woman of incontinence, subsequent to his marriage.[‡]

However, the jury, in the best traditions of English justice, ignored the judge and awarded Duberley £5,000. Gunning later appealed unsuccessfully against the level of damages.

Not everyone in the Gunning family suffered from the trial. Susannah, wrenched from her former domestic comforts and probably in need of hard cash, returned to her former profession of novelist and took full advantage of the new-found notoriety of the Gunning name. On 28 February 1792, the *General Evening Post* advertised her *Anecdotes of the Delborough Family* as 'In press, and will be speedily published'. It weighed in at a healthy five volumes and even healthier fifteen shillings.

Others also saw the possibility of profiting from the General's misfortune, with one publisher advertising a book about the

---

* There seems to have been a deliberate policy by the defence to exaggerate Gunning's age and decrepitude.

† *Town and Country Magazine*, Feb. 1792, p. 54.

‡ *Diary or Woodfall's Regiſter*, 23 Feb. 1792.

Gillray's *Margaret's Ghost,* published 25 March 1791. Margaret Minifie informs her sister (centre) and Elizabeth Gunning of the 'dishonorable-infamous-false-accusations' against them and the 'cruel, most cruel messages that accompanied them'. The original 'Margaret's Ghost' was a ballad written by David Mallet in or before 1724 and appeared in *Percy's Reliques.* A broken brandy bottle lies at Susannah Gunning's feet. Image courtesy of the Wellcome Library, London.

trial with three engravings, one 'A whimsical Representation of the Romp, as acted by General Gunning and Mrs. Duberley, and Mr. Duberley and Mrs. Gardiner.'*

AFTERMATH

Gunning fled the country with Rebecca Duberley† and lived, it was generally assumed, in genteel poverty in Naples.

---

* Classified Advertisement in the *Star,* 28 February 1792.

† Rebecca Elizabeth Howard was born 5 March 1766, the daughter of Gerrard and

Despite publishing a number of successful novels, Mrs Gunning seems to have struggled financially. Perhaps there was some truth in her husband's accusations of extravagance (p. 40).

With her hopes for an advantageous marriage dashed, Elizabeth followed her mother into the writing profession, turning out not only novels but also plays and a translation of Fontenelle's *Conversations on the Plurality of Worlds*.

THE DEATH OF GENERAL GUNNING

The General's health may have been as poor as his counsel had suggested, for he died in Naples in 1797, aged about fifty-seven. Surprisingly, the old soldier does not appear to have been by any means a pauper. The *Chronicle* reported:

> General Gunning, who died a short time hence, altered his Will the day before his dissolution took place, in consequence of a letter he had received from his daughter, Miss Gunning, to whom and Mrs. Gunning, he has left 8,000l., besides his Estate in Ireland to the latter. To Mrs. Duberley he has not left any thing, but to a child he had by her there is a bequest of 1,500l.[*]

Whether or not the General received a final letter from his daughter is not known but most of the paper's information on the will is incorrect. Gunning's will of 16 May 1797 named his wife and daughter as the main beneficiaries and made provision for other relations (including Maria's son, the Rt Hon. George Coventry) and his 'reputed natural daughter Anne Howard (commonly called Anne Howard Duberl[e]y)' by means of an insurance policy on his life. He did not at that time provide for

Ann Howard (baptismal record, 12 March 1766). She married James Duberley at St Anne's, Soho, in 1787 (Pallot's Marriage Registry). The General's will names her as Roberta – presumably a transcription error.

[*] *Chronicle or Evening Post*, 12 Oct. 1897.

Mrs Duberley, except to allow her any surplus from the sale of his continental assets once his debts had been paid. This apparently callous attitude to the woman whose marriage and reputation he had ruined may simply reflect an awareness that her family was wealthy.* However, a codicil of 1 September 1797 does away with the insurance policy, while still providing for Anne, and gives £1,500 to 'my dear friend Mrs Roberta Elizabeth Duberl[e]y'. the will and codicil were proved on 5 January 1798.† Despite the scandal surrounding John Gunning, it appears from his will that he had been promoted as he describes himself as a Lieutenant General.

The value of Gunning's estate is uncertain and it may be that much of it went to pay Duberley's damages for Criminal Conversation. Far from being relieved of their financial worries, both Susannah and, later, Elizabeth seem to have had difficulties making ends meet. Their literary output was quite substantial, but, even so, Susannah was living in reduced circumstances:

> Mrs. Gunning, widow of General GUNNING, has taken the Thatched House at Brompton, lately occupied by Mr. TEXIER, and actually keeps *cows,* for the purpose of supplying her neighbours with *unadulterated milk.* How must the great soul of the departed General, who boasted his descent from CHARLEMAGNE, yearn at the idea of the *industrious humiliation* which his own conduct occasioned.‡

When Mrs Gunning died in 1800, she received more flattering obituaries than either her literary accomplishments or character warranted. She was buried in Westminster Abbey, sharing hallowed ground with Geoffrey Chaucer, Edmund Spenser, Francis Beaumont and many other distinguished writers. Amongst the few lasting memorials to her husband is a chapter

* *Hibernian Magazine,* Feb. 1792, p.161.
† Probate records, National Archives.
‡ *True Briton,* July 1798.

in the *Cuckold's Chronicle*,[*] with the subject matter divided on the contents page, but not the text, into the following sections: Age no security against lust; The sacred deposit; Modern blindman's bluff; Carpet scene; Tea-table etiquette; Wantonness of a mummy.

When she was not engaged in her writing, Elizabeth does not seem to have applied herself to dairy farming but to an altogether different and more dangerous form of employment.

A CAPITAL OFFENCE

The new capital legislation which came into force in 1729 (2 Geo. II c. 25)… was aimed principally at forgers from the respectable classes, people who rarely appeared as defendants in the courts and especially not on capital charges.[†]

Elizabeth was the obvious suspect in the matter of the Blandford forgeries, and later commentators[‡] have not hesitated to condemn her. The evidence presented has been almost non-existent and most of her contemporaries seemed to think her innocent. Without further evidence, there has been no compelling reason to believe Elizabeth responsible for the forgeries. However, there is a clue to her character which seems to have been been completely overlooked.

Mrs Gunning prayed in her *Letter* that her 'innocent darling' be restored to the Duke of Argyll's heart 'in all her *native* truth,

---

[*] Anon, *The Cuckold's Chronicle: being select trials for Adultery, incest, imbecillity, ravishment, &c.*, London: Lemoin, 1793, pp. 79–92.

[†] Clive Emsley, *Crime and Society in England, 1750-1900*, London: Longman, 1996, p. 255.

[‡] With the honourable exception of the *Oxford Dictionary of National Biography* which restricts itself to saying that 'Either Elizabeth or her mother was generally supposed to have committed this grave (indeed, capital) offence'.

simplicity, and *unforfeited* rectitude'.* Until the breaking of the 'Mystery', indeed, there was no suggestion that Elizabeth might have inherited her mother's rather elastic interpretation of the truth. But Elizabeth's later life takes on an entirely different complexion, and one which gives a horrible resonance to her father's† and Captain Bowen's‡ predictions that she would end up in prison.

Elizabeth married Major James Plunkett§ in 1803 and it was under her married name that she made news again:

SALISBURY, *Aug.* 28. On Friday morning, at 6 o'clock, Mrs. Eliz. Plunket [sic] was brought to this city, in custody of Hamilton and another police officer, who had taken her into custody at Collumpton, in Devonshire, on a charge of forgery, and in consequence of 100*l.* being offered for her apprehension, to be paid on conviction. She was met here by her husband, Major Plunkett; and on the officers setting off with the lady for London, the Major followed them in another post-chaise. The hand-bill in which the reward is offered, states that Mrs. Plunkett 'has committed divers forgeries, and among others issued bills on Major Plunkett, her husband, as accepted by him, but which acceptances he denies to be his hand-writing.' It is but justice to add, that we have seen letters from Major and Mrs. Plunkett, wherein they assert that the charges against the lady originated in a very corrupted source, and they request the suspension of public opinion until a trial shall have determined where guilt rests.¶

In September, Elizabeth appeared at Marlborough Street Magistrate's Court in London and looked in real danger of be-

* *Letter,* page 4, Susannah Gunning's italics.
† '... the D—— of ———— would prosecute her and lay her in prison for life,' General Gunning quoted by Margaret Minifie in Susannah Gunning's *Letter,* p. 65.
‡ '... and in *three* days Miss Gunning will be sent to *Newgate*,' Captain Bowen quoted in *Letter,* p. 92
§ Plunkett, of Kinnaird in co. Roscommon, had been pardoned for his part in the Irish Rebellion of 1798. They were married at St George's, Hanover Square on 5 Nov.
¶ *Trewman's Exeter Flying Post or Plymouth and Cornish Advertiser,* Thursday, 31 August 1809.

ing convicted and hanged for forging a number of bills. Fortunately for her, friends (or possibly embarrassed aristocratic relations) made a proposal to the complainant, a money-lender called King, who agreed to drop the case on 13 September:

> Mr. NEAVE, the magiſtrate, said, when the documents in queſtion were the second time before him, he could not avoid perceiving that if the charge were to be persevered in, the transaƈtion would be found to amount to a felony of a capital nature. It was fortunate for the lady that these documents had remained in Mr. King's hands; had they got into those of a third party the consequences might have been fatal. As Mr. King was now satisfied, however, and there was no prosecution before him, he had nothing farther to say.
>
> Mr. ADOLPHUS* hoped after the humanity which Mr. King had shewn to the unfortunate lady, that her friends would not undertake any vindication of her innocence in the public, which might produce irritation, and prove equally fatal as if the prosecution were now to proceed.
>
> Mrs. PLUNKETT, on being discharged out of cuſtody, made a courtesy and retired.[†]

Elizabeth had escaped the gallows for now, but it was not long before she was facing further charges. On 19 October, she and her husband returned to Marlborough Street Magistrates Court:

> *Major Plunkett* was on Wednesday charged, at the suit of Mr. Northwood, of Molineaux-ſtreet, Mary-le-bone, with forging an acceptance to a bill of exchange purporting to be of the value of 65*l.*; and *Mrs. Plunkett*, who was some time since charged with forgery at the suit of Jew King, was charged with uttering the said bill of exchange, knowing it to be a forgery.
>
> The prosecutor said that he received the Bill of Mrs. Plunkett, a twelvemonth since, but on presenting it, the drawer could not be found, and having paid it away, he afterwards paid the value of it. He had called upon Major Plunkett, who denied that it was his acceptance, but

* Representing Mr King.
† *Morning Chronicle,* Thursday, 14 September 1809.

observed that he did not chuse to lead his wife into a snare by answering the queſtion in any shape. Witness had no idea that the bill was a forgery, until he conversed with Major Plunkett.[*]

It sounded very similar to the first case, with Elizabeth apparently issuing forged bills of exchange and her husband denying all knowledge of them. This time, however, Major Plunkett was also in the dock. Mr Parker, a solicitor, told the court that the charges were without foundation. He laid out the defence case as follows:

… previous to Miss Gunning having been married to Major Plunkett, she was pressed for money, and Mr. Northwood, the prosecutor, had discounted bills for her, for which he always received a valuable consideration. After Miss Gunning's marriage with the Major, she, unknown to her husband, sold an annuity of 50*l.* per annum to the prosecutor for 180*l.* she being then ſtill pressed for money. The Major, on becoming possessed of the faɛt, offered to repurchase the annuity, and pay five per cent. for the use of the money advanced. There was a balance of money due from Major Plunkett to the prosecutor, which the former was willing to pay. The prosecutor refused to settle the accounts, and said he would arreſt the Major. Mr Parker ſtated, that he had several interviews subsequently with the prosecutor, who said, that if the Major did not pay him the whole sum due to him, he would take up his wife for forgery.

Mr. PARKER contended, that he never heard a syllable about forgery until Major Plunkett refused to comply with paying the sum of money Mr. Northwood required, which was about 400*l.*

The Magiſtrate asked Mr. Parker, if he was ready to swear, that in his several interviews with the prosecutor, he had never heard about a forgery until Major Plunkett refused to pay him his alleged balance?

Mr. PARKER replied, that he was ready to do so at that moment.[†]

As a result, Major Plunkett was discharged. However, Elizabeth still faced charges and was bailed to reappear at a later

[*]   *Examiner,* Sunday, 22 Oɛtober 1809.
[†]   *Examiner,* Sunday, 22 Oɛtober 1809.

date. When the case resumed, and further evidence was given, the magistrate, Mr (later Sir Nathaniel) Conant stated that:

> ... he was bound to send the matter to a Jury in a superior Court, who could alone be competent to decide upon the guilt or innocence of the prisoner. A felony was diſtinctly and positively sworn to, by a respect-able witness, againſt Mrs. Plunkett. But though no discretion on the point was within his authority, he would do anything within his power to obtain her liberation upon adequate sureties. He therefore advised Mr. Praker [sic] to lay a proper affidavit before a Judge, with such oth-er evidence as he could obtain; which, backed by his own (the Magis-trate's) recommendation, he had little doubt would obtain the libera-tion of Mrs. Plunkett on good bail. In the mean time she should be treated with the utmoſt tenderness, and might be indulged with the company of her friends in a private room, under the care, however, of a Police Officer. Mrs. Plunkett seemed extremely grateful for this indul-gence* and remained in the private chamber of the Magiſtrate, while her solicitor proceeded to adopt the advice he had received; but failing of that, she was committed to Tothill-fields Bridewell.[†]

However, by the time that this report appeared, she had al-ready been bailed.[‡] On Monday, 13 November 1809, it was re-ported that, despite convincing evidence of her guilt, a grand jury had thrown out the charges against her.[§]

In the light of these prosecutions, it is hard to resist the con-clusion that Elizabeth was also behind the forged letters at the heart of the the so-called Gunning Mystery.

---

* As well she might. Mr Conant seems to have been almoſt as charmed by Eliza-beth Plunkett as Mr Juſtice Caulfield was by Mary Archer at the trial of her husband when he asked 'Has she elegance? Has she fragrance? Would she have, without the ſtrain of this trial, radiance?'

† *Ipswich Journal*, Saturday, 28 October 1809. Tothill Fields was a prison in the city of Weſtminſter. Bridewell, the name of the infamous London prison near the church of St Bride, Fleet Street, was used as a generic word for a prison, especially a place of forced labour.

‡ *Hampshire Telegraph and Sussex Chronicle*, Monday, 23 October 1809.

§ *Hampshire Chronicle*, Monday, 13 November 1809.

An Apology for the Life of
MAJOR GENERAL GUNNING

HOWEVER humiliating it may be for me to expose the picture of my life, and a series of events marked with folly and extravagance, I can no longer sit down contented under a load of obloquy, and see my errors deepened into their darkest shade, when a candid explanation may, perhaps, extenuate my guilt, and wipe off some part of that censure which has been wantonly cast upon my name. The envious and ill-natured disposition of one half the world is but too often employed to disturb the peace of the other. Man is at war with man from the moment of his birth, and seems only to rejoice when an opportunity offers to lessen his reputation, and ruin the tranquillity of his mind, I have suffered much from this unnatural and inhuman propensity. It is in vain that the dissipations of the world concealed from my eyes the defects and follies of my heart; they were marked, scrutinized, and censured by mankind; and at a moment when I least expected such a blow, a thousand friendly hands were stretched forth to tear off the dressings from my wounds, and expose them to the air in cruel fits of diversion. It is not sufficient that my follies have been shewn to the world in their darkest colours, they have been multiplied and blackened; and I have no other resource left to quiet the solicitude of my heart, than to appeal to the humanity of that world by which I have been already, perhaps, prejudged.

It is but too often the custom of persons who plead in their own defence, to cast a veil over their follies, and, while they admit the predominancy of a vice, lay its foundation on a virtue.

But with me this vanity has ceased to please. I ask neither applause nor admiration. I write not to justify, but extenuate; and as I mean not, in the recapitulation of my life, either to gratify the impertinent curiosity of the vulgar, or subject my actions to the false conclusions of the ignorant; I shall but slightly touch upon the many years of my life which were thrown away in the frivolous pursuits of folly and extravagance, and hasten on to that period when my actions and principles wore the air of mystery to the world, and become suspicious even in the eyes of my friends.

I am now arrived at that period of life when nothing can soften the reproaches of a broken heart but a sound and upright conscience, which the mortifying reflections of my own mind tell me I do not possess. – Let this confession silence the asperity of slander; and the picture of a debilitated old man, struggling with the accumulated inconveniencies of sorrow, sickness, poverty, and distraction, repress the triumph of successful villainy. – I shall cease to blush at the remembrance of my follies, if the relation of them can open the eyes of the rising generation, and teach them to shun the errors into which I have fallen.

It would be superfluous to mention my birth and splendid connexions. The world is already acquainted with my origin, and the means by which those accumulated honors that dignified the female branches of my family were obtained. The beauty of my sisters was for years the theme of admiration, and it is no wonder it raised them from a state of dependence to grace the first dignities in the kingdom. Their beauty and situation were unequalled, and under the flattering auspices of their protection I was first introduced to the world. A scene of prosperity and pleasure now seemed to open on me, of which the less auspicious years of my early life had given me no anticipation. The pursuit of pleasure was the only business I engaged in, and the moments seemed to glide away without a care to interrupt them. – I saw myself courted and admired on every hand; the men prevented my desires of pleasure by new scenes of dissipation, and the women exempted my heart from the little pangs of doubt and expectation by granting their favors almost unsolicited. – While I was thus employed in imbibing these intoxicating pleasures, I had neither time nor inclination to examine the situation of my affairs. My expenses far exceeded the income of my estate, which scarce amounted to five hundred pounds per annum, and was left at the death of my father charged with a mortgage of four thousand pounds, besides a number of less considerable debts. It is true, the affluence and affection of my sisters left me no reason to complain of pecuniary embarrassments: but their generosity was exceeded by my extravagance: and I often repined and cursed my fate, in the midst of the most promising scenes of prosperity, for not rendering me capable of enjoyments, which, but a few years before, my most extravagant ideas could have formed no conception of, and would have appeared, had they been depicted, like a vision to my mind. From hence I may date all the succeeding misfortunes of my life.

The dissipation of these hours sunk deep into my heart; and neither a sense of its impropriety, age, nor poverty, has been able to divest it of its fascinating complexion, and wipe it from my mind.

The beauty which exalted and aggrandized one part of the family has been the ruin of the other. Had my sisters never possessed those infatuating charms, I might have been happy in the inheritance I was born to enjoy, and sunk into my grave without the curses of injured virtue on my head: but the fatality of their perfections, which drew me into the vortex of dissipation, was intended for my destruction; and I now feel the full force of those evils I have so often despised.

My conduct now became more and more culpable. The most eccentric absurdities and extravagancies filled up the measure of my days, and my nights were marked with abominations too horrid to repeat. No violation of morality was too shocking to be performed; – no scheme of perfidy too dark to be embraced: when my friends, alarmed at the dissipated course of life I was leading, and apprehensive of the ruin which threatened me, procured me a commission in the army – in hopes a change of place and difference of society might cure me of my extravagance. But this was only removing me from the stream to the fountain head. I had before tasted of folly; but here I drank my fill, and was initiated into the more refined mysteries of the debauchee. I now despised my former superficial knowledge of iniquity, which had been gleaned in the brothels, gaming-houses, &c. in the metropolis; and sat down to study methodically *a system of seduction*, &c. which had been laid down for the instruction of military novices. I made a rapid progress in this delightful science, and, joining practice to theory, passed the time allotted for my probation with great *eclat*, and was at length esteemed one of the most successful and strenuous supporters of the society.

My library chiefly consisted of such books as tend, to vitiate the mind, and debauch the understanding. *L––d C–––––d's Letters*[3] and *C––––––a H––––––w*[4] were generally my morning's amusement. From the former I learnt all the arcana and inexpressible refinements of a man of intrigue, and from the latter all the principles and practice of an accomplished. v–––n.[5] The spirit of *L–––––ss*[6] took possession of my bosom; a congeniality of sentiment and coincidence of desires made me in love with his character, and I could not help admiring a picture which bore so strong a resemblance to myself. *Alexander the Great* could not esteem the *Iliad* more than I did these *precious volumes*. They were, my study by day, and my pillow by night; and as *Alexander* endeavoured to form himself on the model of *Achilles,* so I pursued the more pleasing though not less arduous task of imitating the *divine Loveless.*[7] My success was equal to my most flattering anticipations. My desires were scarce excited before they were gratified; and I might ten times in twelve stand over the ruins of the virtue I had destroyed, and exclaim with *Cæsar,* VENI, VIDI, VICI.

My hours now passed away on the golden wings of love: every night brought its pleasure, and every day happy reflections on the past, or joyful anticipations of the future. *Debauched, false,* and *dissembling,* under an air of mildness and timidity I concealed the most dangerous and vicious passions, and every hour was devoted to perfect myself in the art of dissimulation, and the most successful methods of ingratiating myself with the women, that I might render them subservient to my pleasures. I found the air of ingenuous modesty I had assumed was the most seductive snare; it procured me confidence and esteem, and an opportunity of taking a thousand little liberties with almost every woman, which tended to excite her passions without alarming her delicacy.

I very soon learnt that the rude and impetuous blunders of forward impudence never fail to disgust. To publish your intention is to place a woman on her guard, and to leave her in full possession of her reason to oppose and circumvent your designs. The road to success is much more easy, though less perceptible. It consists in a thousand little inexpressibles utterly incomprehensible to a vulgar mind, and is made up of all the insinuating relatives of tenderness, deference, and adulation. These intoxicating offerings, as efficacious as the sop of *Cerberus,*[8] charm the dragon *Honor* to rest, and open the way to victory and pleasure.

It is a matter of astonishment to me, that the generality of men should be so shamefully ignorant of human nature, as to misconceive their duty so grossly in this particular. To imagine the voice alone has the power of seduction is ridiculous – 'Tis the eyes, 'tis the soul which must speak through them, that can convey the pleasing infatuation. What a want of knowledge in this branch of commerce a man betrays, says *Sterne*,[9] who ever lets the word *love* come out of his lips till an hour or two at least after the time that his silence upon it becomes tormenting! – *A course of small quiet attentions, not so pointed as to alarm – nor so vague as to be misunderstood – with now and then a look of kindness, and little or nothing said upon it – leaves Nature for your mistress, and she fashions it to her mind.*

This is the only true definition of that part of the art of insinuation called MAKING LOVE, that ever I met with. It is the precept of nature as well as the seducer, and has, when put in practice, conquered the pride and insensibility of many a heart that no other method could subdue. A man must STOOP *to conquer*,[10] and must FALL to *rise*. It is but the debasement of a moment, and the hours of pleasure that follow it are surely a sufficient recompense for his temporary submission.

I have had innumerable opportunities to observe the little prejudices and dispositions of the female heart. I know the falsehood, the dissipation and eccentricities that are engrafted there, and how few are devoted to promote the felicity of a man who is incapable of making them any return by contributing to their interest or their pleasure, or even the gratification of their vanity. They must be soothed and flattered to their ruin. There is something so shocking in the consequences of seduction to a female mind of any delicacy, that it requires the utmost ingenuity to conceal the snare, and play with the passions, till reason has no longer the power to oppose you.

An apparent modesty, joined with an insinuating aspect and a melodious voice, is the most dangerous weapon of a designing man. Women cannot endure us when we demand their approbation as our due, and look as if we would bully them into a compliance with our desires. The great business of their life is love, and the disposal of their hearts the principal incident in their history. It is not wonderful, therefore, that they look upon every incitement of passion as a matter of such moment, and require us to accept their hearts as the most peculiar favour. Besides, there is a pride and pleasure in conferring an obligation highly flattering to their vanity; and they are naturally inclined to love those whose meekness and submission give them an opportunity of exerting their power, and enjoying an imaginary triumph.

The lesser arts of insinuation are known to almost every man, and practised upon almost every woman. The common-place method of complimenting their understanding, and their beauty, and their taste, and their follies, and their vices, &c. &c. is all very deceitful, and of course very pleasing; neither is the more expensive method of making presents to be despised. Women are in general pleased with toys, and men lose nothing by their their liberality in this particular; for *Shenstone*[11] justly observes, the making presents to a woman one addresses, is like throwing armour into an enemy's camp, with a resolution to recover it.

I must here observe, that the common-place observations of moralists upon the vicious appetites of men, and the virtuous inclinations of women, are equally false and ridiculous. The one are neither so faultless nor the other so guilty as they are represented. The levity, indiscretion, and, perhaps, indelicacy of the women are the principal source of their misfortunes. Their reliance on their own prudence is the rock on which they generally split; and the sentiment, that a woman may allow all innocent freedoms provided her virtue is secure, is both grossly indelicate and dangerous, and has proved fatal to many of the sex.

That confident ease and unabashed countenance, which seem to set the world at defiance, and which the ladies have adopted to complete the hostile appearance they take so much pride to betray, are as disgusting to a man of sense and delicacy of feeling, as that indiscriminate attention, that unmeaning simper, which smiles on all alike, and arises either from an aukward affectation of softness and susceptibility, or a perfect insipidity. One of the chief beauties in the female character is that modest reserve, that retiring delicacy, which avoids the public eye, and is disconcerted even at the gaze of admiration. I do not mean to insinuate that an insensibility to applause is amiable and praiseworthy. That would be to be devoid of feeling, which is one of the loveliest ornaments of the sex; but there is a medium to be observed, which every woman of penetration may easily discover.

An air of modesty is the most insinuating address; and if a woman knew the value of such a charm, and the power it would give her, she would not barter it for all the affected airs, delusive glances, and wanton lisps of the most accomplished coquette.

The power of a fine woman over the hearts of men, and of men of the finest parts, is inconceivable; and even beyond the flattering representations of her most sanguine hopes. They are struck with love and admiration, and a thousand agreeable emotions of tenderness and passion overwhelm their minds: they see the delusive path they are pursuing, and are sensible of the illusion that misleads them, but they cannot, nor do they wish to dissolve it. But if she is determined to dispel the charm, neither the magic of her beauty, nor the infatuation it inspired, can prevent it; and she may soon reduce the angel to a very ordinary girl.

A fine woman, like all other fine things in nature, has her proper points of view, from which she may be seen to most advantage. To fix this point requires great judgment, and an intimate knowledge of the human heart. By the present mode of female manners, the women seem to expect that they shall regain their ascendancy over us by the fullest display of their personal charms; by a little licentiousness of conduct and expression; and by priding themselves on the imitation of our most culpable eccentricities. But a very little time and experience will shew the folly of this expectation.

Women are little aware of the jealousy of man, and how satirically he comments upon every the smallest deviation from those bounds which are laid down as the only proper sphere of their action. The most innocent expression is obnoxious to perversion; every look, every motion, has its signification; and the most ill-natured constructions are put upon every action that is open to a false conclusion.

A woman must be strangely infatuated indeed, who thinks to recommend herself to our sex by an almost total renunciation of her own. – THE AGE OF CHIVALRY IS GONE. Our modern race of heroes do not hold it necessary to go forth on romantic expeditions of knight-errantry, to bring home proofs of their valour to lay at the feet of their mistresses; nor to see the object of their adoration armed cap-a-pee,[12] ready to put their courage to the test, and dispute every inch of ground before she yields up the possession of her person. If the blood of *Alexander* no longer animates the veins of one part of the creation, the heart of the *Amazon* should cease to beat in the other.

We so naturally associate the idea of female softness and delicacy with a correspondent delicacy of constitution, that the want of it is disgusting in the extreme, and a proof of that hard and masculine spirit, which of all a woman's faults we dislike the most.

When a girl ceases to blush, she has lost the most powerful incentive of passion, and the most alluring charm of beauty. – That extreme sensibility which it indicates may be a weakness and incumbrance in our sex, *as I have often felt;* but in hers it is peculiarly engaging. Pedants, who think themselves philosophers, ask why a woman should blush when she is conscious of no crime? It is a sufficient answer, that nature has made her to blush when she is guilty of no fault, and has forced us to love her because she does so. – Blushing has been called the robe of virtue; and is so far from being necessarily an attendant on guilt, that it is the usual companion of innocence.

The world may probably smile at reading lectures of this nature from the pen of a *professed* ––––––: but it should be remembered, that folly has no longer the charm for me it once possessed. I am not now drawing the outlines of intrigues which I have not the power to accomplish, nor writing precepts of seduction in the profligate spirit of youthful iniquity. My intention is only to point out the errors into which I have fallen, and the rocks on which I split. Should others be tempted into these dangerous paths, they may learn from my example to shun my evils; and, by attending to what I write, may hear, for once in their lives at least, the genuine sentiments of a man who has no longer any interest in flattering or deceiving the world.

From the very early opportunities I had of learning the false and hypocritical spirit of mankind, I have been in a state of warfare with the happiness of the whole universe almost ever since my birth. And what is there in the society of so depraved a world, that I should be tempted, for its sake, to mortify my senses, and give up their sweetest gratification to its felicity and ease? All the people I see, are too much engrossed by schemes of interest or ambition, to have any room left for sentiment or friendship. Conversation is reduced, to party disputes, and illiberal altercation; and social commerce sullied with envy, malevolence, and intrigue. Every person you deal with endeavours to over-reach you in the way of business; you are preyed upon by sharpers and idle mendicants, who pick your pockets *for the love of God*, and live upon the spoils of the stranger. Your tradesmen are without conscience, your friends without affection, and your dependants without fidelity. The most innocent man, in appearance, is generally the greatest rogue; and in the end proves either a tartar, a spy, or a lunatic.

In such a world, what has a man to do with honesty? The thought of such universal depravity is a comfort to me in my present dejection, and an alleviation to those bitter reflections which sometimes shoot across my mind. But I have done with the science of men; and though my natural inconstancy of disposition, and love of dissipation, may sometimes transport me into the vortex of folly, I shall only return with a more complete contempt of one part of the world, and detestation of the other. Every thing that is to be seen, and heard, and felt, in that reservoir of knavery, falsehood, and sophistication, is only a greater inducement to the mind to detect, and renounce it for ever.

But it is time that I should turn from general to particular vices, and recall to my mind those scenes of dissipation which employed the most considerable part of my life.

I have already said, that gallantry was the great object to which all my thoughts, studies, and accomplishments were directed; and here I might gratify perhaps the curiosity of one part of the world, and the malevolent disposition of the other, by relating the history of the numberless adventures I have known in the course of my pleasures; but at present I am not disposed to furnish food to either the licentious or splenetic blockhead, and shall only relate such anecdotes as please my own fancy, without studying to gratify an ungrateful world, to which I owe nothing but hatred and detestation.

It is certain that a man of parts, sentiment, and address, if he lays aside all regard to truth and humanity, may engage the hearts of fifty women at the same time: it is therefore no wonder that, afflicted by their own love of admiration (which by the bye has been the ruin of thousands of women of the best hearts, and the finest accomplishments), I should triumph over the virtue of almost every woman I assailed.

In a practice of forty years and upwards, I have scarcely known what it is to fail in a single instance; and have during that period enjoyed the favors and full possession of the most accomplished and lovely women of the age. And even now, emaciated, crippled, and worn out as I am with length of years, debauchery, and disease, there are women, devoid of neither youth nor beauty, who hear my voice with admiration, and behold my person with desire.

It was not sufficient that, in the course of my amours, I should have women to gratify the desires of my sensuality. My heart was too delicate to yield itself to any thing but the impression of beauty in its most lovely shape; and however my appetite might have been palled by continual enjoyments, my taste remained pure and unsullied.

The gratification of sensuality alone never gave pleasure to my heart. I required a softer interest, a more intimate connexion with the object of my desire, than ever I could form with women who were not eminently blessed with the fascinating power of personal perfection. Nothing but beauty could infatuate and attach me; and to possess it, I have suffered as many changes, and metamorphosed myself into as many shapes, as ever *Proteus* assumed. No difficulty, no obstacle could impede my desires;

and the absurdities I have committed to accomplish my ends are almost incredible.

As it suited my convenience, I have been an atheist and a devotee – a philosopher and a rake – a parson –a player – a cynic, a conjuror – a patriot – a courtier – a footman – a moun-tebank – a pedlar – a mendicant and a prince – and almost every other character that is to be found in the extremities of human nature. – I have been of all religions, and of all sects – I have kneeled with the Roman catholic at the figure of her saint, and cursed with the pious protestant, in the devotion of my heart, all idolatry and superstition. – I have raised my voice with the violent declaimer of eternal damnation, and- have groaned in spirit, and professed charity towards all mankind, with the self-humiliated quaker. – I have renounced the articles of faith, and talked of predestination; and have broke of the bread and drank of the cup of the modest puritan. – Nay, I have been drenched in a consecrated horse-pond, for the sake of a pretty anabaptist; and actually suffered the pain of circumcision, to obtain a fair jewess, who possessed some of the *prettiest diamonds* and sweet-est features that ever I met with in any one woman.

It is not to be wondered at that, among such a variety of characters, I should have tasted all the richest enjoyments sen-suality can bestow, and been pretty deeply read in the preju-dices, follies, dissipations, and irregularities of the human heart.

Let the dull and unimpassioned moralist enjoy the felicity of virtue, and spend a life of serenity and peace in the undissipat-ed shades of monastic glooms. I envy him not the philosophic tenor of his mind, the dull sensations that preserve him from the temptation of pleasure, nor the pulse that vibrates but with the motion of a heart which is regulated by the calm influence of sanctity, stupidity, and superstition. With a soul devoted to pleasure, I have flown, not struggled through the world; and now, standing as I am upon the very extremity of human nature, I cannot keep my eyes from turning back to gaze upon the lovely phantoms of those scenes, which continued in a most beautiful succession from the morning to the meridian of my life, and still shine with almost undiminished lustre on the evening of my days.

I thought my repentance of folly had been sincere; but I find it impossible to destroy the temper of the mind. Images once impressed upon the memory will be rising of themselves from time to time, though we give them no encouragement; as the tossings and fluctuations of the water continue several hours after the wind is laid.

Human nature cannot abide long in the game humour; and those that seem to be always even-tempered people, like the *Caspian* sea without ebb or flow, are only counterfeits and politicians. There is an art to conceal one's passions, but there is none that can annihilate them. We change from one affection, appetite, and desire to another. Our inclinations circulate with our blood: they are transformed each minute, hour, and day; and are as fickle as the winds of heaven.

I am convinced it is vain to struggle against the disposition that nature has given us. The efforts of virtue on a depraved mind are too often faint and ineffectual; and all its effects are discoloured and tinged with the darkened shades of the heart. The stream cannot be pure when the fountain is polluted. The strange infatuation of vice is almost incredible; and where folly has once let its impress, neither time nor reason can eradicate its features from the soul. It is recorded of *Barbara* the empress, wife to *Sigismund,* another *Messalina,* that after her husband's death, her confessor advising her to reform her manners and live more chastely, like the turtle, she answered, 'If I must imitate the life of birds, why not a *sparrow* as well as a turtle?'[3]

But to return from this digression. To give a perfect relation of all the intrigues in which I have been concerned, and the little anecdotes annexed to them, would require volumes; and I intend to throw away but a very few pages in the events of a life which is scarcely worth recording. I shall, however, slightly touch upon some circumstances that have made a deeper impression than others; and among the rest shall submit to the world the following list of women, whose virtue was not proof against the united efforts of *opportunity* and *importunity*.

I shall give these ladies, not according to the several periods at which they were devoted to my pleasures, but according to their rank in the world; that their pride at least may be preserved inviolate, however their reputation may have suffered by the event.

Two Duchesses – One English, and one French.

Fourteen Countesses – Five English, two Irish, one French, and six German.

Four Viscountesses – All British.

Seven Baronesses – Three English, two Scotch, and two Irish.

Baronets' Ladies, thirteen – Seven English, four Scotch, and two Irish.

Lord Mayors', Knights', and Aldermen's Wives, five – All British.

'Squires' Ladies, twenty – Mostly British.

Peers' Daughters, *unmarried,* fourteen – English, Scotch, and Irish.

Descendants of Peers, *in the third and fourth generation,* twenty-one – Ditto, ditto, ditto.

Young Ladies, *without any pretensions to nobility*, twenty-seven – English, Irish, Scotch, French, Dutch, and Americans.

Maids of Honour, five – All British.

Old Maids, one – Strong Spanish, with a dash of the Irish and Scotch.

Undistinguished Widows, eleven – Of all countries, and of all ages and descriptions.

Thus the sum total of my amours, as nearly as I can calculate, amounts to sixty-six married women; sixty-two virgins; five maids of honour, who are neither one thing nor the other; one old maid; and eleven widows; in all, amounting to the grand sum of One Hundred and Forty-five Persons.[14]

My descendants are almost as numerous as my conquests; many of them I never saw, but those which I know of may come under the following description, *viz.*

Two Cardinals,
One Bishop,
One Duke,
Four Earls,
Two Viscounts,
Six Barons,
Nine Baronets,
Two Lord Mayors,
Two Aldermen
One Sheriff,
Nineteen Esquires,
Three Physicians,
Seven Barristers,
A Dissenting Parson,
A Jewish Rabbi,

A Trading Justice,

A Republican,*[15]

Twenty-four Younger Brothers,

Thirty-seven Non-descripts,

And Eleven German Counts, every one of whom has killed his man, to prove the purity of his blood, and the antiquity of his family.

I have not here mentioned any of my progeny in the female line. It is very extensive, I believe; but as I never had either any inclination or opportunity to enter into the merits of these ladies, I have by neglect entirely forgot their number, as well as their virtues. My family is, however, as numerous as I could wish; and though I am sensible I must have made some few omissions, as my account at present stands, my striplings of iniquity amount to the number of One Hundred and Fifteen.[16]

Were I to relate the various methods, schemes, and hypocritical pretences I made use of to insure me success in the course

---

* This fellow, of all my descendants, is the one I moſt dislike. He is the crude fruit of an old maid (vide the catalogue *de mes petites Méchantes*) begotten in disguſt, and brought forth in a fit of the spleen. The world may be surprised, perhaps, that I could so far conquer the delicacy of my taſte, as to submit to a connexion of so diabolical a nature; but it was a case of compassion, of caprice, of fickleness, or of what you will. I wanted, in short, to break the pride and subdue the prudery of such an animal, and to see what the offspring of so ſtrange a concatenation would produce; but I have paid severely for my curiosity, by giving being to a dogmatical cynic, that has been peſtering the world with his schisms and quibbles ever since he could snarl. This *extraſt of verjuice* seems only to delight in the contempt of the laws, the ruin of nations, and the rooting up of monarchies; and we may say of him, as some wit said of the famous Dr. Kenrick, 'He drinks *aqua-vitæ*, and spits *aqua fortis*.' The fellow appeared in the world at firſt with a tolerable share of *Common Sense*, but it has all evaporated, I fear, in his ridiculous fables of the *Rights of Man*. I will not venture to prophesy his exit from the world; but as he was begotten and came into it with infinite Pain, it is probable, if he meets his deserts, he will leave it with sensations of a similar nature.

of my amours, mankind would regard them with equal astonishment and admiration; but such a recapitulation is but little
adapted to the present situation of my mind. – Suffice it therefore to say, that my principal care was to blend together the most
striking parts of the three following characters – the Hero, the
Gentleman, and the Petit-maître.[17] In the study of these parts
I found all the accomplishments necessary to polish the mind,
adorn the person, and give all *eclat* to the most simple and un-
premeditated actions.

In the character of a hero, I assumed an air of confidence
and superiority; swaggered, fought, and conquered. – Under the
name of a gentleman, I wore an appearance of modesty and as-
surance, which claimed both attention and respect. And with
the frivolous *badinage* of a petit-maitre, I softened both the austerity of the hero and the reserve of the gentleman; and related
the common-place chit-chat of the day with such pretty tones
and such insinuating looks, that I have often been attended to
with admiration in these empty rhapsodies, when virtue and
good sense have been totally disregarded.

In the character of a petit-maitre a man ever appears to the
best advantage in the eyes of a woman. It is an imitation of
herself, and never lays a man under the imputation of being a
conjuror; though it requires a considerable degree of knowledge
and acuteness to perform it with dexterity. In this character I
have sported away many hours of my life, and received more
smiles than ever shone upon me in any other situation.

I have wantoned round a lady's toilet, with all the antics of
an amorous monkey, for hours together, I have disposed her
curls, her patches, and her pins. I have suited her ribbands to
her complexion, and sometimes her complexion to her ribbands.
I have criticised on muslins and cambrics for an hour at a time,
and given a lecture on the properties of ice-cream and whipt-

sillabub to admiration. I have divided her dress into a hundred parts, and given her the history of each particular; describing her muff and fan as coming together from the different ends of the earth – her scarf from the torrid zone, her tippet from beneath the pole – her brocade petticoat from the mines of *Peru,* and her diamond necklace from the bowels of *Indostan.* I was always perfectly instructed in the follies and fashions of the day; knew every minute circumstance of every domestic tiff, every fashionable *faux pas,* and could tell to a nicety the dress of the most fanciful lady, the airs of the most affected gentleman, and the form, history, and dimensions of every new trinket, &c.

These things will of course appear trifling to a person who is unacquainted with their influence on the female sex; but still they are the most important points of learning to a man of intrigue; and as necessary to be acquired before he can take his degree in the court of Love, as ethicks are to a doctor of divinity, before he is approved by the university of *Cambridge.*

'No flattery,' says Lord *Chesterfield,* 'is too gross for a woman to swallow;' and he might have added, no trifling too insignificant to delight her.

As a proof of this, I beg leave to mention a circumstance which obtained me the possession of the countess of ––– when the most ingenious devices had failed, and at the very moment she was in the zenith of power, and beheld every eye sparkling with love and admiration of her beauty.

I had watched the glances and gratified the desires of this lady for above a month together, with as much solicitude and devotion as a pilgrim at the shrine of his saint; but this elevated beauty was as deaf to my felicitations, as any saint in the calendar to the oraisons of enthusiastic folly. I had exhibited all the little hypocritical arts of insinuation in vain; when one day, tired and chagrined at her indifference, I caught her little favorite child to my breast, and lavished those kisses upon his lips which I would fain have imprinted upon his mother's. The countess's eyes sparkled with delight as I embraced her child; but when she saw me take my handkerchief from my pocket and wipe his nose, which was dirty, she could no longer contain the tenderness of her heart. I beheld her delight with the most triumphant satisfaction; and, taking her at the critical moment, pleaded my cause with so much passion, tenderness, and persuasion, that she had not power to withstand me, and I was gratified to the utmost extent of my desires. Thus wiping the wet nose of a squalling little brat, gained me the possession of the finest woman in Europe.

Before I relate any of those little histories of my amours which I intend to throw into this work, I must observe, that the stigma usually cast upon a woman whose passions prompt her to deviate from the path of rectitude, partakes in a great measure of that malevolence and spirit of satire that almost every creature in the universe levels against another. People seldom trouble themselves with more than a superficial view of things, and too often pronounce judgment without entering into the merits of the cause.

How often is a woman bound by the chain of matrimony to a man, whose every idea, word, and action, is a wound to the feelings of her heart! Instead of meeting with sense, delicacy, and tenderness; a lover, a friend, and a pleasurable companion in a husband, she may be tired with dulness and insipidity; shocked with indelicacy, or mortified by indifference. Thus situated, she will find none to compassionate, or even understand her sufferings. The world will laugh at her delicacies, and call her objections chimerical; but should she take the law into her own hands, and revenge herself for the infidelity of her husband, and reap that pleasure her parents denied her, by giving way to the tenderness of her heart, the world immediately loathes the sound of her voice, and shuts her from its society. Her footsteps are marked with pollution, and the very air she breathes is looked upon as contaminated. 'Whip me such stoics, Great Governor of Nature!'[18] and give me rather to wear for ever the yoke of bondage on my neck, than the weight of such fetters on my soul!

I, who was never an advocate for matrimony, still look upon it as the most abominable species of slavery; and in the younger part of my life thought it a virtue to divert the melancholy moments of those whose inauspicious stars had placed them under its malignant influence.

Among the many occurrences I have experienced of this nature, I cannot avoid the temptation I feel to relate the following story:

Some years ago, when I was in *America*, I was introduced one evening at a hall to a lady, whose beauty, tone of voice, and expression were the most infatuating that can possibly be conceived. My heart did not remain a moment insensible to her perfections. The instant that gave her to my eyes impressed her image on my soul; and the conversation of a few minutes so entirely captivated me, that she could not but discover the almost universal agitation I was thrown into whenever our eyes encountered each other. The hours seemed to glide imperceptibly away while I hung in a fit of transport on the music of her tongue; and when the moment of our separation arrived, I thought I beheld a melancholy thoughtfulness in her aspect, which seemed to express all the tenderness I could wish for.

I handed her to her carriage; and when I pressed her hand at bidding her adieu, she softly returned the pressure with a blush of timidity which so entirely fascinated me, that I had not the power to move from the spot till some time after her carriage had vanished from my sight.

It was in vain I endeavoured to close my eyes, and flatter myself with future opportunities of accomplishing the desires of my heart. The thought of her husband's watchfulness, who I had learnt was jealous of her to distraction, disturbed my repose, and placed so many obstacles in the way of my felicity, that the night was passed in the utmost torment and agitation.

In the morning I formed a thousand romantic schemes to ingratiate myself with the husband of my mistress; but the surly and jealous disposition of the brute rendered them all impracticable. For about a fortnight I remained in the most tormenting perplexity, being deprived the whole time of the sight of my lovely inamorata. At length, however, the idea occurred to me of engaging myself in her service, and I put it in execution in the following manner:

I sent for her footman, and, pretending that I knew some of his connexions, offered to take him into my service as my valet-de-chambre, and make his salary much more considerable than I knew the profits of his place at that time could possibly amount to. The fellow immediately closed with my proposal; gave in his resignation, agreeably to my desire, and entered upon his new employment the same day.

Thus far my success was as splendid as I could wish. My next care was to procure leave of absence from my regiment, which I easily obtained; and telling my servants I was going for some time to a distant part of the country, ordered a few articles of linen, &c. to be packed up and conveyed to a place I had provided for the purpose; then dressing myself in a suit of plain clothes, I proceeded to the house of my little idol; and, having obtained admission to the presence of her husband, offered myself to him in quality of a lacquey.

This gentleman eyed me with the most suspicious penetration; but as there was nothing in my appearance he could possibly object to, after catechising me with respect to the history of my life (with the simple circumstances of which, as I related them to him, he seemed perfectly satisfied), and examining one or two discharges I had taken care to provide for the occasion, he condescended to honor me with his approbation, and clothe me in the tinsel livery of my obsequious valet,

The novelty of my situation was extremely pleasant; and the thought of attending my mistress at all hours, and the happiness that such an adventure might in the end procure me, made me particularly active and attentive to the duties of my function.

The same day I entered on my new employment gave me the opportunity I so long desired, of gazing upon the beauties which had made so deep an impression on my heart. This angel, for so she certainly appeared in my eyes, entered the dining-parlour, attended by her husband; and glancing her eye slightly, upon me as she passed, blushed, and, turning away her head, applied her handkerchief to her face to cover her confusion.

This adventure disconcerted me a little; but I was sufficiently master of myself to conceal my emotions, and to wait at table with an air of the most perfect *nonchalance*. But my mistress was not quite so much at her ease. She trembled whenever I approached her, and avoided, as much as possible the meeting of my eyes. She spoke little, ate less, and complained of indisposition and a depression of the spirits, to avoid exciting suspicions in her husband; who frequently enquired into the cause of her silence, and the variation of her countenance, which was alternately spread with the most fascinating blushes, and the more tempered shadows of modesty and confusion.

To describe the situation of my mind after I left her presence, and during the whole of the succeeding night, would almost be impossible. I was agitated with the most tormenting passions, the most lively anticipations of felicity, and the most afflicting doubts and apprehensions; but in the morning I was resolved to push my fortune as far as it would go, and leave the rest to fate.

I accordingly wrote to the object of my desire in the most passionate and insinuating terms I could invent. I depicted in the most lively colours, the affection I had conceived for her, the pleasure I experienced in the few hours I was permitted to enjoy her conversation, the grief that seized upon my heart at the moment of our separation, and all the various afflictions I had sustained from that to the present moment. I pointed out the romantic hopes of happiness I had conceived, in being permitted to gaze upon her, in the tenderest language; and begged, since she was devoted to the arms of another, and fate had deprived me for ever of the sweet hope of being united to her, that she would not debar me of the only happiness I could enjoy, that of waiting and gazing upon her.

This letter I contrived to deliver secretly to my lovely mistress during the time she was at breakfast; and, as I attended her in the evening, had the happiness to receive an answer from her, couched in the most delicate and expressive terms.

She pitied the excess of my passion, chided me for my imprudence, hinted at the infelicities of her own situation; yet intreated me, if her happiness was dear to me, to give up the romantic idea of continuing as her domestic; as it might probably expose us both to the revenge of a man, whose implacability of temper would leave us no room to hope for mercy or compassion.

If there had been any doubt of her triumph over my heart before, this letter would have completed her conquest. My passion was now at its height. I wrote to her again, and obtained her permission to continue in the quality of her footman; and as we had but few opportunities of convening together, we kept up this little epistolary correspondence, and mutually exchanged letters every day.

My assiduity and attention in my official capacity was extremely pleasing to my master, and I ingratiated myself so much into his good graces, that he looked upon me as a fellow of the utmost fidelity. He sometimes condescended to honor me with his confidence; and the familiarity of his behaviour soon removed all that restraint which the nature of my situation, and the consciousness of my intentions, had at first oppressed me with.

Every day now softened the asperity of my master's conduct, and every hour gave me opportunities of beholding and conversing with my lovely mistress. It is but natural to suppose, that a man of my complexion did not throw away these important moments. They were employed in the most delightful science, and the desires of my heart were at length crowned with all its fondest wishes had anticipated; But fortune, who had long indulged me in her choicest pleasures, was now resolved to change the scene, and make me pay a dear price for the gratifications I had enjoyed.

After I had a long time tasted the most delicious fruits of my victory, we were one day surprised, in the midst of our tendered caresses, by the unexpected approach of my master, who coming directly to his wife's apartment, just allowed me time to creep under the bed. The disorder in which he found his wife might have alarmed a less jealous temper; but she might easily have excused her déshabille, and evaded his suspicions, had he not, by a cross accident, discovered my legs, which the time had not allowed me to conceal in a proper manner. He immediately seized me by the ankles, and drew me out into the middle of the room; then turning to his wife with a stern countenance, and snatching a short sabre that hung at the head of his bed, would have instantly dispatched her, had I not very gallantly seized his arm, and with many imprecations asserted her innocence and my own guilt; which, however, I protested had hitherto, gone no farther than design. She so well seconded my plea, that he was at length imposed upon; and now all his rage was directed against me. Simple death he looked upon as too small a punishment, and seemed to rack his brain for some new and unheard-of torture to inflict upon me, which the poor lady was in too great a fright to dissuade him from executing; and perhaps, if her concern for me had made her attempt it, it would have raised a jealousy in him not afterwards to be removed.

All the servants in the house were by this time collected in the chamber; and my master, pleased with the cruel suggestions of his own mind, ordered me to be seized and bound, swearing that he would do severe justice on me for my criminal intention, and prevent me from any danger of executing my wicked purpose hereafter.

I was at first so shocked at hearing my barbarous sentence pronounced, that I had not power to oppose the decree; and was very near seeing myself, like poor Abelard, bound to the stake, and deprived of all pretensions to manhood.[19] But returning to myself at the moment of my destruction, I leaped from the grasp of my assassins, and, seizing a red-hot poker from the fire, brandished it over my head with the most determined ferocity, and with a few sweeps of my weapon left all my antagonists sprawling on the ground. I did not pause a moment to triumph over the fallen; but locking the door after me, to prevent the possibility of pursuit, I stripped, off my livery, and, returning to my lodgings, assumed once more the appearance of a military man.

Thus ended an adventure that had afforded me some of the most delightful hours I had ever experienced; and in spite of the inconstancy of my nature, I could not reflect upon moments that had been sweetened with the caresses of so angelic a woman without a sigh of regret; and to ease my heart of reflections which destroyed its felicity, I attached myself to a little *French* coquette, whose beauty and eccentricities were at that time the theme of admiration.

This lady was of that class of volatile spirits which the *Spectator* so admirably ridicules under the name of *Idols;* but as there are a great variety of these pretty saints, it is justly observed, that it would be as difficult a talk to reckon up the different kinds of these images of idolatrous worship, as Milton was to number those that were known in *Canaan,* and the lands adjoining.

Most of them are worshipped, like *Moloch,* in fires and flames; Some of them, like *Baal,* love to see their votaries cut and slashed, and shedding their blood for them; and some of them, like the idol in the *Apocrypha,* must have treats and collations prepared for them every night. Their humour and extravagance are prettily described in a tale of Chaucer. He represents one of them fitting at a table with three of her votaries about her, who are all of them courting her favor, and paying their adorations. She smiled upon one, drank to another, and trod upon the other's foot, which was under the table. Now which of these three, says the old bard, do you think was the favourite? In troth, says he, not one of all the three.

My lively *Parisian* was exactly of this disposition; and the sequel of the story will prove how little the fidelity of a coquette is to be depended upon.

At the time I first marked her out as the object of my pleasures, she was surrounded by at least a dozen men, to every one of whom she had given the most flattering encouragements, and reason to hope the full gratification of his desires. But I, who saw through the wantonness of her disposition, and the pleasure she took in exciting the jealousy, and tormenting those who had imprudently declared their attachment to her, piqued her pride, and played off with her own weapons to so much admiration, that she would have given the world to subdue an indifference which seemed to set her art at defiance. In vain she practised all the little wiles of coquetry and dissimulation; I maintained my ground with the most philosophic resolution, and baffled by the most provoking extravagancies all her stratagems of insinuation. Every hour seemed to draw forth some new caprice in my character. – Alternately tender and indifferent, I caressed her at one moment, and neglected her the next. I was now all life and spirit, and now sullen and unentertaining. With a countenance of sorrow and dejection I would cast myself at her feet, and entreat her, in an ironical tone of voice, to compassionate and reward the tenderness of my affection. In short, I tormented her so completely, that, to be revenged of me, and at length to have the pleasure of a triumph, she gave me the opportunity I had waited for with so much anxiety, and gratified both her own pride and my pleasure at the same moment.

This intercourse lasted for some time, and would probably have continued much longer, had not a little accident interrupted our pleasures, and put an end to our connexion.

One evening, on my return from a party in the country, with which I intended to continue a few days longer than I really did, I proposed to myself the pleasure of going to her house about midnight, and surprising her with my presence. I entered by a little garden-door, of which I had the key, and proceeded without any noise immediately to her chamber. But what was my surprise at beholding the little infidel in the arms of my own footman, whom I had permitted, at her request, to continue with her during the time I was in the country!

My astonishment deprived me of all power of utterance for the moment; but recovering myself, I tore the miscreant from the bed, and was proceeding to handle him very roughly; when, without appearing in the least disconcerted, my little traitress told me, she was amazed at my impertinence at taking such liberties with any person under her protection and gave me to understand, that she had only indulged me with the possession of her person to gratify her own pride; that the novelty of our connexion was now wore off; that she had pleased her own inclination in giving way to the passion of my valet; and concluded with begging me to depart in peace; intimating, at the same time, that she must otherwise be under the necessity of collecting her servants, and giving them orders to dismiss me out by the window.

During this pretty harangue, I had time enough to collect my thoughts, and resolution enough to despise her; so giving her shivering paramour a hearty kick or two as I retired, I made my exit, and left her to the enjoyment of her lover.

This adventure occasioned me so much chagrin and ill-will towards the whole sex, especially that part which takes pride in coquetting and sporting with the feelings of every man, that I denounced war against them without mercy; and carried on my conquests with so much rapidity, that I had scarcely time to reap the fruit of my victories.

In the earlier part of my life I had the timidity of a novice about me, in spite of all my inclination to succeed, and the examples I had daily set before my eyes by the industry of my companions; but I was now tolerably well versed in the hypocrisy of the men, and the weakness of the women, and joined to a prepossessing appearance, a most invincible desire to possess every woman eminent for her beauty and accomplishments.

To account for my extraordinary success is impossible, and it appears at this moment a mystery to myself. I have sometimes, merely to try how-far the language of persuasion on one side, and the weakness of nature on the other, would prevail on a woman, sat down to study the temper of a mind, and indulge it in all its extravagancies; and though I have had no other desire but curiosity to gratify in such an attempt, I can scarcely remember a single circumstance of this nature, in which I have not been obliged to yield to the temptation of seduction to preserve my own reputation.

Whatever visions of virtue philosophic apathy may invent, they can make no impression upon my mind, while the experience of sixty years and upwards,[20] supported by every faculty I possess, rise up in judgment against them. Honor in the possession of a woman, as one of the sex has observed, melts like ice-cream in the mouth: and I would as soon trust to the tenets of *Mahomet,* as to my grandmother's proving virtuous against a temptation of vice.

I was once told by a woman, who was by no means remarkable for her deviations from rectitude, that she had repeatedly endeavoured to assume the prim air of virtue, and stifle every emotion that was not strictly conformable to its dictates; but she candidly acknowledged that she was always baffled in the attempt, and never had the power to hold out against the temptation of pleasure for three hours together. Virtue in a woman is certainly nothing more than the *sal mortuorum* of the ancient Romans, whose beams served only to give a faint mock-glimmering to the ghosts that wander on the side of *Charon's* ferry, and like an *ignis fatuus* to mislead them up and down in the dark suburbs of *Elysium.*

It is prettily observed, and justified by experience, that the virtues of man are written in sand, and the record of his perfections may be destroyed by the first blast of the zephyr; but that his vices are engraven on tablets of brass, and are never to be expunged. The latter, like the heads of the *Hydra,* shoot forth with new vigor as soon as they are destroyed: but the vital spark of the former may be extinguished in a moment; and not unaptly compared to the *Venetian* treasure; which being once shewn to the *Spanish* ambassador in many coffers of silver, gold, and jewels, the wife *Castilian* desiring to see the bottom of these wealthy chests turned up, when it was done, made this remark – *Your riches have no roots, nor grow, like those my master doth possess in the Indies.*[21]

The boasted excellencies and acquisitions of morality are much of the same nature. No traditional chemistry of men can revive the soul, or call forth a virtue from a heart tinged with vice, and branded with imperfection. Perhaps some theological *Paracelsus, Helmont,* or *Arabian Ifriqui,* may from the ashes, of an original flower raise the fantastic form of it again, that is, the colour and contexture of the leaves; but none of them is able to bestow the vital sap, the seminal juice, the inward virtue of the once prosperous and flourishing vegetable. No mortal can repair what *Adam* once destroyed. That *Protoplast* and his *wife* have ruined us all.

I have sometimes myself, in the midst of my most licentious scenes, sat down to examine and imitate the boasted loveliness of virtue; and in one of these fits actually resolved to renounce my follies, and marry some little *ignoramus,* whose fortune might enable me to live like a gentleman, and repair the former extravagancies of my life.

In this idea, I made my first addresses to a young lady in the country; and things went on most swimmingly, till the old put,[22] her father, happening to hear that I had been strongly suspected of *crim. con.*[23] with the Countess of ————, forbad me his house, and within a fortnight after gave his daughter, with twenty thousand pounds, to a roaring fox-hunter in the neighbourhood.

I made my next applications to a widow, and attacked her so briskly, that I thought myself within a fortnight of her. As I waited upon her one morning, she told me that she intended to keep her ready-money and jointure in her own hands, and desired me to call upon her attorney, who would adjust with me what it was proper for me to add to it. I was so rebuffed by this overture, that I never enquired either, for her or her attorney afterwards.

A few days after I addressed myself to the most innocent-looking little creature in the universe. I danced with her, sung to her, told her pretty stories from the Fairy Tales, squeezed her hand, said all the soft things I could invent, and gained her permission to open the affair, to her father. But as I went one day to the house in order to break the matter to him, I found the whole family in confusion; and heard, to my surprise and morti-fication, that Miss *Louisa* had that very morning run away with the butler, by whom she had been with child six months before.

After this I laid siege to four heiresses successively, and was as happy as I could possibly wish in their good opinion; but I don't know how it came to pass, though I seldom failed of get-ting the daughter's consent, I could never in my life get the old people on my side.

My next attempt was highly promising of success; and I should certainly have accomplished my point at last, with a very pretty brunette, and a splendid fortune, had I not been fool enough to put her virtue to the test. – I pressed for a premature enjoyment, and she had not the resolution to oppose me. In short, she admitted me to her bed the night before we were to have been married, and my *honor* would not permit me to unite myself to her after such a *faux pas*. This was the dearest plea-sure I ever enjoyed. – Her fortune was at least thirty thousand pounds.

My last effort was upon an old woman eaten up with the gout, palsy, and a strong asthmatic cough, whom I had certainly borne away with flying colours, if her relations had not come pouring in to her assistance from all parts of *England;* nay, I believe I should have got her at last, had she not been suddenly carried off by a hard frost and a violent fit of the cholic.

My want of success in these arduous undertakings disgusted me so much, that for that time I gave up all thoughts of matrimony; and joining the companions of my former pleasures, I bound my temples with chaplets of myrtle and roses, as the merry fellows among the ancients are described,[24] and fought once more the smiles of dissipation; or, to express it more delicately in the words of Monsieur de *Fontenelle, – des graces qui rient, et des amours qui folâtrent.*[25]

It is in scenes of this kind alone that the source of pleasure is observed never to grow dry; in all other situations of life there is some little drawback on our felicity, some perplexing circumstance which destroys our prospect, inverts the mirror, and shews the dark shade of the picture to the eye. But in the happy vacuity of thought, and variety of pleasures, which dissipation procures, a man has not time to grow stupid in his enjoyments. His desires and gratifications almost accompany one another, and leave him no room to repine in that expectation of pleasure, which the dilatory tempers of women very often excite in the more calm and retired scenes of the world.

This tormenting propensity in women is most admirably rallied in the *Spectator,* where a brother of the coif[26] complains, that he began his suit *vicesimo nono Caroli Secundi,*[27] before he had been a twelvemonth at the *Temple;* that he prosecuted it for many years after he was called to the bar; that at present he is a serjeant at law; and not-withstanding he hoped matters would have been long since brought to an issue, the Fair One still *demurs.* This spirit of demurring seemed to prevail so much at that time, that another gentleman declares, that he had been playing bo-peep with his mistress till she had grown as grey as a cat, had not a tooth in her head, and was changed from a pretty hoyden of a girl into a good motherly sort of a woman. And I actually knew a lady myself, who permitted a man to court for one-and-twenty years before she consented to marry him, and had deferred it for fourteen years, as she afterwards declared, merely because she could not prevail upon any of her young married friends to let her into the secret of such a connexion.

Ladies of this disposition should recollect, that life is not long enough for a coquette to play all her tricks in. A timorous woman drops into her grave before she has done deliberating. Were the age of man the same that it was before the Flood,[28] a lady might sacrifice half a century to scruple, and be two or three ages in demurring. Had she nine hundred years good, she might hold out to the conversion of the *Jews,* before she thought fit to be prevailed upon. But, alas! she ought to play her part in haste, when she considers that she is suddenly to quit the stage, and make room for others.

This is a maxim I have ever preached, and ever practised; and in the hey-day of my blood, I looked upon a day's loss in matter of intrigue, with as much regret as the Emperor of *Rome* expressed, when once recollecting he had done no good action during the day, he laid his hand upon his breast, and exclaimed, *I have lost a day.*

My anxiety to employ my hours in the earlier part of my life, was so very great, that I had frequently two or three affairs of gallantry upon my hands at the same time; but this is an ambition I would not advise every man to covet, as it is attended with a considerable degree of danger and perplexity. The tormenting jealousy of a woman who imagines she has a right to your person, is putting her continually on her watch; and if she discovers the smallest infidelity on your part, she either persecutes you with her complaints and suspicions, or invents some diabolical method to be revenged. I have had frequent apprehensions of entangling myself in these snares, and occasion for all my ingenuity to silence the jealousy of one, counteract the coquetry of another, and stifle the tormenting fondness of a third.

This infidelity and dissimulation in a man is certainly imprudent, if not culpable. It exposes him to a thousand little inconveniences that are inconceivably distressing; and the woman that can contrive an innocent method of revenge for such inconstancy, is certainly to be admired.

I met with a little story of Monsieur *Pontignan*[29] the other day, which sets this matter in so pleasant a point of view, that I cannot help quoting it, and shall give it to the reader in the words I find it translated to my hand.

When I was in the country, says he, last summer, I was often in company with a couple of charming women, who had all the wit and beauty one could desire in female companions, with a dash of coquetry, that from time to time gave me a great many agreeable torments. I was, after my way, in love with both of them; and had such frequent opportunities of pleading my passion to them when they were asunder, that I had reason to hope for particular favours from each of them.

As I was walking one evening in my chamber, with nothing about me but my night-gown, they both came into my room, and told me they had a very pleasant trick to put upon a gentleman that was in the same house, provided I would bear a part in it. Upon this they told me such a plausible story, that I laughed heartily at their contrivance, and agreed to do whatever they should require of me. They immediately began to swaddle me up in my night-gown with long pieces of linen, which they folded about me till they had wrapt me in above an hundred yards of swathe: my arms were pressed to my sides, and my legs closed together by so many, wrappers, one over another, that I looked like an *Egyptian* mummy.

As I stood bolt upright upon one end in this antique figure, one of the ladies burst out a-laughing: 'And now, *Pontignan*,' says she, 'we intend to perform the promise that we find you have extorted from each of us. You have often asked the favour of us; and I dare say you are a better bred cavalier than to refuse to go to bed to two ladies that desire it of you.'

After having stood a fit of laughter, I begged them to uncase me, and do with me what they pleased. 'No, no,' say they, we like you very well as you are and upon that, ordered me to be carried to one of their houses, and put to bed in all my swaddles.

The room was lighted up on all sides, and I was laid very decently between a pair of sheets, with my head, which was indeed the only part I could move, upon a very high pillow; this was no sooner done, but my two female friends came into bed to me in their finest night-clothes,

You may easily guess the condition of a man that saw a couple of the most beautiful women in the world undrest and a-bed with him, without being able to stir hand or foot. I begged them to release me, and struggled all I could to get loose; which I did with so much violence, that about mid-night they both leaped out of the bed, crying out they were undone. But, seeing me safe, they took their posts again, and renewed their raillery.

Finding all my prayers and endeavours were lost, I composed myself as well as I could; and told them, that if they would not unbind me, I would fall asleep between them, and by that means disgrace them for ever. But, alas! this was impossible; could I have been disposed to it, they would have prevented me by several ill-natured caresses and endearments which they bestowed upon me. As much devoted as I am to woman-kind, I would not pass such another night to be master of the whole sex.

My reader will doubtless be curious to know what became of me the next morning. Why, truly, my bed-fellows left me about an hour before day, and told me; if I would be good and lie still, they would send somebody to take me up as soon as it was time for me to rise: accordingly about nine o'clock in the morning an old woman came to unswathe me. I bore all this very patiently, being resolved to take my revenge of my tormentors, and to keep no measures with them as soon as I was at liberty; but upon asking my old woman what was become of the two ladies, she told me she believed they were by that time within sight of *Paris,* for that they went away in a coach and six before five o' clock in the morning.

Such was the mortifying end of poor Monsieur *Pontignan's* amours; and I think the ladies, whoever they were, ought to be immortalized for their happy invention, and resolution in putting their stratagem in execution.

This story puts me in mind of an adventure that once happened to a brother officer of mine, who paid his court to a most beautiful woman, and withal a coquette of the first order. My adventurous friend was of the most diminutive size, and his mistress, on the contrary, so very tall, that when they appeared together, they were no bad resemblance of the caricature of the sexes in disguise. After a very long attendance, &c. my little hero at length prevailed on his mistress to gratify his desires; but in a *nota bene* to the articles of capitulation she had the wickedness to insert the following malicious clause: *That, before she surrendered, their great toes should be tied together.* I need not add that this article entirely ruined the project.

This species of coquetry may be very entertaining on the one side, but is certainly very perplexing on the other, as indeed I

have sometimes experienced. I remember I once attached myself to untractable spirit (for she could not bear the gross idea
of having any thing of the animal at all about her) that was all
sentiment, soul, and sublimity. This, if I may be allowed the expression, was the *gamut* of her passions; and she would play me
as many tunes upon these three words, as Handel himself ever
drew from the keys of a piano forte.

Her pretty lips were continually uttering precepts of morality; her soul recoiled at the most distant idea of sensual pleasure; and I have seen her almost in a fit of hysterics at the bare
thought of the smallest connexion between the sexes. She had
written an essay upon the generation of the vegetable world, and
used continually to lament the death of some ancient natural-
ist, whose laborious studies had once discovered a more innocent way of propagation for the Human species; but, it seems,
his tables, unfortunately falling into his wife's hands, the gross
creature, alarmed at the doctrine they contained, threw them
into the fire.

This little visionary kept me in play for some time; but I at
length found means, in one auspicious moment, to overthrow
her principles; and destroy her whole system of self-denial at a
blow.

In casting my eye over what I have written, I find I have indulged myself much longer than I intended in relating some of
the scenes of the former part of my life; but it is now time that
I should put an end to such trifling, and enter upon a history of
events of a much later date, and by which the curiosity of the
world has been excited.

It cannot have escaped the reader's observation, that, in the
picture of my life, I have omitted the representation of one object,
which is generally esteemed the principal figure in a domestic
drawing: I mean my wife. This solecism in point of attention is

not to be imputed to any want of respect towards that lady. My *dear Mrs. G———* knows that I have the utmost veneration for her virtues, and the tenderest affection for her person: but after the commission of so great a folly as matrimony, the best thing a man can do is to cast a shade over it, as Ham and Japhet did over the nakedness of their father, and conceal it if possible from the knowledge of the world. It is now too late, I confess, for me to screen myself, beneath such a cloak. Mrs. G——— has already published our union to the world, and I might justly be accused of rudeness and want of gallantry, were I to deny a connexion with so *charming* a woman. Her sprightly wit has beguiled the insipidity of many an hour (for she certainly is a woman of *extraordinary* genius, though she has the modesty to deny it); and it is to her happy invention and romantic enterprises that I may attribute the downfall of my family, and the honour I have acquired in becoming the laughing-stock of the nation.

It would be impertinent in me to repeat the well-told story my dear Mrs. G——— has already given to the public; but it may not be uninteresting to make a few comments merits upon it, and rectify some little mistakes which crept into it, and still wear an air of mystery to the world.

Mrs. G———, in her relation of those strange circumstances which blew up the credit of my house, forgot to mention that they originated in the pride and ambition of her own heart. She forgot to observe, with what a world of endearments, and, if I may so say, what a *cataract* of eloquence she, upon my appointment to the command of a regiment, pointed out the increase of my revenue, and the splendors that ought to encircle, to use her own expression, a general of the first magnitude. She forgot to declare, that these and the like solicitations drew me from my retirement in the country, into the vortex of fashion, and placed me in an elegant house in St. James's Place, with a new equipage set forth in the most modish style, and a crowd of valets, grooms, and lacqueys of every description.

Thus far the desires of this amiable lady were accomplished; but as she wisely foresaw a scene of such splendor could not be long supported upon the profits of a regiment (my estate being long ere the period I am speaking of mortgaged for very near its value), she resolved to make the most of her daughter's beauty, and confirm the dignity of her family by the same means that it originally acquired its most peculiar marks of distinction.

With this praise-worthy intention, Miss G————, drest as fine as a little princess was sent to court, and introduced it all the fashionable routs and hurricanes in town; with strict orders from her prudent mother to avoid all acquaintance and familiarity with gentlemen beneath a certain rank, and not to dance, ogle, or even permit her little finger to be prest by any person that was not heir-apparent to an earldom at least.

These injunctions were, I believe, strictly adhered to, and seemed to meet with tolerable success; for Mrs. G————, drawing me aside one morning, with the most fascinating vein of pleasantry and good humour let me into the whole of their plan, and set it in so plausible point of view, that I looked upon the thing as already done; but when she told me, a few days after, that my daughter had made a complete conquest of her cousin, the Marquis of L ————,[30] that mutual declarations of fidelity had passed between them, and that, in short, there was nothing but the Duke of A————'s[31] consent requisite to put the last hand to the business; I was elated with the most auspicious anticipations of joy, and could not help saluting, my dear Mrs. G————'s *immaculate darling*, as the future Marchioness of L————.

I was naturally anxious, to learn the progress of this amour, which seemed to promise so much prosperity to my family, and was not a little surprised to find that an entire change in the business had taken place in the course of a few days; that the Marquis of B————[32] had been put in opposition to the Marquis of L————; and that it was a point not entirely decided upon between the ladies, which of the two Marquisses should be honoured with the preference. As this was a matter of etiquette, in which they insisted I had no right to interfere, I gave up the point; only begging that I might have the earliest intelligence of their choice.

Matters continued in this situation for some time, when I was given to understand that the Marquis of L ————, who it was at length agreed upon should be accepted, was not so urgent in the business as formerly; that it would be, therefore, necessary to encourage the Marquis of B————, in order to awaken the jealousy of his rival, and by that means bring the affair to a happy and speedy conclusion.

As this was an innocent piece of coquetry, I thought it very advisable to put it in execution, and a strong flirtation, as I was informed, immediately commenced. The plot now began to thicken, and the *denouement* to take place. The Marquis of L———— was still backward, and there was only one way to bring him to the point desired; and that was, according to my dear Mrs. G————'s opinion, to write a few passionate epistles to her daughter, with the signature of the Marquis of B————, and dispose of them in such a manner that they might fall into his rival's hands, and thus leave him no alternative.

I was now too far engaged in the business to recede, or boggle at trifles; I therefore gave my consent and assistance in the affair. The letters were written in Mrs. G————'s best manner, and might probably have met with the most flourishing success, had not some evil spirit counteracted our design, and, by conveying some intimation of the plan to the Marquis of B————, ruined the whole project at a blow.

The matter now became the chit-chat and theme of scandal of every fashionable tea-table in town. It was canvassed by persons of every description; sarcasms made their appearance as periodically as the newspapers of the day; and I found it necessary to make some grand effort to extricate myself from the business, and preserve my reputation unsullied.

For this purpose, I summoned a grand council of the whole family; and it was unanimously agreed upon, that I should pretend ignorance on the occasion – look upon the Marquis of B————'s imaginary proposals as having actually taken place – and write to the Duke of M———— for an explanation of his son's conduct. We easily foresaw that an ecclaireissement of this nature would open the eyes of the world, and occasion a total revolution in the family: But this we were content to bear – it was only for me to renounce, *in appearance,* my wife and daughter, and keep the secret on which all the politics of our little commonwealth depended. Affairs being thus settled, every thing was performed according to agreement; and I need not tell the world, that the result of my application to the Duke of M————, was a positive denial of the knowledge of any intended connexion between the families on his part, and an absolute refusal of my daughter on that of his son.

There was now only one part of our project unexecuted, and that I very soon performed, by turning, in a *seeming* rage, my wife and daughter out of doors, as it had been previously agreed upon in full Diet. This motion completely puzzled the wiseacres of the town; who now unanimously pronounced in my favor, and imagined I had been as egregiously imposed upon as they actually were. But, though I had thus secured my own reputation for the present, I soon found it necessary to compound the matter, with my amiable spouse, who felt a little impatient under the obloquy and ill-natured insinuations of the world, and intimated her; resolution of publishing the *whole* truth, if I put in the smallest objection against her palliating and softening the matter in the prettiest manner she could. This would have been *confusion worse confounded*, and adding to the criminality of the business with a vengeance; I was therefore obliged to give her a *carte blanche*, and full permission to blacken my character as much as might be consistent with her plan, provided only that she did not touch upon the *real* truth of the affair; and it must be confessed that she has handled her pencil with the utmost dexterity, and laid on her colours with a most liberal hand.

With respect to the introduction of Captain and Mrs. B———,[33] and the part allotted them in this business, I cannot help saying but that I think my dear Mrs. G——— is a little too severe. She should have remembered that I had no power over the reputation of my friends, and that my permission to indulge her fancy on this subject was not meant to extend any farther than the limits of her own family. This gentleman and lady ought to have been sacred: they acted as friends to the family, and * *
* *
* *
* *
* *
* *
* *
* * * * * * * * it was certainly very unmerciful in Mrs. G——— to treat them with so much cruelty, after having given us these proofs of their friendship, and inclination to promote our welfare.

I have thus explained this seeming mystery, not much to my own credit, I confess; but I have no longer any interest in deceiving the world, and look upon its applause, at present, as of very little consequence to my peace. Mrs. G———— may plume herself upon the chastity of her diction, and the novelty of her style, which is certainly well calculated to set off a bad cause; but I hope I shall not be less credited in a *round unvarnished tale*,[34] that cannot boast the aid of such brilliant ornaments.

I have now only one more adventure to relate ere I close the scene of my life; and I could have wished that the evening of my days had not been marked with an event, that even *I* cannot survey without some bitter reflections on the depravity of human nature.

When I obtained the command of the ———— regiment[35] in the beginning of the year 1788, I first became acquainted With Mr. D————[36] of Soho-square, who undertook to clothe it for me upon much more liberal terms than any other person in his line of business. The polite attention of this gentleman was highly flattering to a man of my disposition; and as I foresaw his purse might prove very serviceable to me in case of necessity, I took care to cultivate his friendship with the utmost solicitude.

My endeavours were not thrown away. Every attention on my side was repaid with politeness and hospitality on his, and in a short time I beheld myself on a very familiar footing, in his house. Upon my coming to town and settling, in St. James's Place, a more intimate connexion took place between the families. The ladies visited; and as often as the gout and a complication of other disorders would permit me, I used to lounge away the morning in chatting with Mrs. D————, whose beauty, youth, and sweetness of disposition were eminently calculated to please a man of my taste.

This connexion was, for a long time, perfectly innocent on my side. I had a desire to possess her, it is true; but as I was then reduced to my crutches, and scarcely able to hobble from one end of the room to the other without assistance, I had not the vanity to believe that the persuasion of my tongue, however practised in dissimulation, could ever seduce a woman who had scarcely attained her twentieth year, from the arms of one of the handsomest men in London, to caress me in age and decrepitude, and *with all my imperfections on my head*. But yet, in spite of these disadvantages, which would have been sufficient to discourage any other man, and my inclination to be virtuous for once in my life – that depravity of mind, and libidinous turn of my affections, which united to betray me, from almost the first hour, of my existence to the present moment, into some criminal extravagance or another, soon conquered the faint efforts of expiring virtue, and left me a prey to the most ungracious and seductive passions that ever disturbed the peaceful tenor of the heart.

Worn down, diseased, and decrepit as I was, I had not the strength to subdue the importunity of my desires, or banish the language of seduction from my tongue; But in the midst of these detestable emotions, my thoughts were diverted from the object of my pursuit, by the perplexing circumstances of my daughter's amours, the happy effects of my dear Mrs. G————'s fruitful invention.

The result of that business reduced me to the greatest extremity. The report of the revolution that had taken place in my family had scarcely reached the ears of the public, but my tradesmen came flocking in from every quarter, and demanded payment of their several debts. Money I had none – my estate, as I have already observed, was mortgaged till it would mortgage no more – my *noble* friends, my *dignified* relations, all looked upon me as an injured man, and pitied, most *sincerely* pitied my case. They advised me to let my house, dismiss my servants, and discharge my debts; but it was *unfortunately* a time of the year when their rents did not become due, And they of course could not oblige me with any pecuniary assistance; the want of which entirely ruined the project their good advice had laid for my advantage; for I could neither leave my house, dismiss my servants, nor discharge my debts.

In this dilemma I had no other alternative than to apply to the usurers, Jews, and pickpockets of the town. These gentlemen's proposals were as liberal as one might expect from the villainy of their profession. They we're to supply me with eighteen hundred pounds to silence the most clamorous of my creditors, and allow me an annuity of three hundred pounds, for which they were to receive the full profits of my regiment; amounting upon an average to *Nine Hundred Pounds* per annum.

When the instruments which were to deprive me for ever of the income of my regiment were prepared, and I was on the point of signing them, Mr. D———, whom I affected to treat with the utmost confidence, shocked at the ruin which threatened me, took the pen from my hand, and declared his resolution to supply me himself with any money I might have occasion for; and, calling my creditors together, paid them their demands, to the amount of *Two Thousand Pounds*.

As this gentleman had done me one kindness, he was resolved not to leave me till he had rendered my situation as comfortable as possible. He accordingly dismissed my servants, and disposed of my house; and as I was then in the most deplorable situation, and tormented with the most afflicting diseases, he invited me to Soho-square, and permitted me to continue in his family for near two months, till I was sufficiently recovered to bear the fatigue of moving, and a comfortable lodging had been provided for my reception.

It may be justly said, that a life of gratitude, devoted to the service of such a man, could scarcely repay him for such exalted and disinterested friendship; but my heart, shut to the tender feelings of humanity, and hardened in the most depraved scenes of the world against every sentiment of gratitude, sought but the gratification of its own unjust desires, and means to accomplish the infelicity and dishonour of my benefactor.

Mrs. D———'s politeness and good-nature made her very often sacrifice engagements of a more agreeable nature to the pleasure of being my companion, during the time I resided in Soho-square; and I was too well versed in the art of insinuation not to improve those moments to the utmost advantage. Strange as it may appear, I found her heart by no means invulnerable; and in a very short time saw my diabolical designs attended with so much success, that her reluctant virtue yielded to the force of my persuasion, and in one moment I levelled all those flattering hopes of happiness which her husband had promised to himself in the entire possession of her affections.

Mr. D———, little suspecting what serpent he was fostering in his breast, still continued his attention to my ease and welfare, and gave me a general invitation to his house, where I used constantly to dine &c. when I had no particular engagement elsewhere, I was by this means enabled to indulge my passion for Mrs. D——— in all its licentiousness, and repay the friendship of a man I was bound almost to adore, with the grossest violations of beneficence and hospitality.*

Blest, if I may so say, in the last scene of my life, with the caresses of a woman formed to fascinate the soul, my felicity knew

---

* The treatment this gentleman received at my hands cannot perhaps be better exemplified than by repeating the complaint of a poor Swiss, who had been repaid for his hospitality to an ungrateful soldier, by the commission of the crimes enumerated in the following simple though expressive tale, pronounced before the delinquent in the presence of his officers. 'May it please your honors, dis shenteman come into, my house – he eater my meat – he drinker my drink – he picker my purse – he ***** my wife – he b**ger mine eyes – and he kicker me down ſtairs!'

no interruption and when Mr. D————'s family removed for the summer to their house at East-Sheen, I still found myself a welcome guest, and used regularly to make one of a party every Sunday at his table. As Mr. D———— was generally at home all day on Sunday, my opportunities of holding any particular conversation with his wife were very confined; but as he used to drive to town on Monday morning with rather more expedition than I did, it was my custom to let him pass me on the road; and, after we had saluted each other, to order my carriage to wheel to the right about, and bear me back to the arms of my impatient dulcinea.

In this manner I used to enjoy the most delightful pleasures; but the impossibility, as I thought, of being discovered, rendered me imprudent, and I had very nearly exposed myself to the thing I most dreaded by a too frequent repetition of these visits.

One day in particular, while I was indulging myself as usual, Mr. D———— was seen riding towards the house, and had, by the time he was first observed, approached so near as to prevent the possibility of an escape. My situation at this alarm was inconceivably distressing; but my dear little friend, with infinite presence of mind, instantly summoned her confidential maid, and, delivering me to her care, ordered her to disguise me in any manner she could invent, to prevent my person from being known.

This faithful abigail immediately led me to the nursery, and in less than two minutes huddled me into a brown camblet gown, an old ragged petticoat, a coloured apron, a greasy silk handkerchief, and a mob cap. – Thus equipped, I seated myself in an easy chair, with a young child on my lap, in the character of the nurse's mother, and, with a pap-spoon instead of a truncheon in my hand, waited the approach of the enemy.

The deception took to a miracle. Mr. D——— came into the room, and, little imagining a general officer of Great Britain could be disguised in the shape of an old woman, passed without the smallest suspicion; and as soon as I received intelligence that he was safely seated in the parlour, I submitted to be led in this horrid trim, like Sir John Falstaff in the Merry Wives of Windsor, through the blind corners and back stairs in the house, till I came to a postern gate, and got into an unfrequented lane, where my carriage used always to wait upon these occasions.

This, though a perplexing circumstance, was not the only one I endured during my visits to Mrs. D——; for I was once tumbled headlong into a meal-tub, and looked when I was drawn forth again as white as a miller; and another time, being wrapped in a foul clothes-bag, and kept there for three hours, was almost suffocated for want of air.

These things, though disagreeable in themselves, were sweetened, and rendered even pleasant, by the caresses and participation of the person that occasioned them. – But the hour was now approaching when the peaceable possession of these pleasures was to be disturbed, and the sweet indulgences of my former life rendered the tormentors of every future day.

Not to keep the reader long in suspense, it is only necessary to observe that Mr. and Mrs. D———were to go in September last on a visit of a month or two, at some considerable distance from town, and that I had prevailed on Mrs. D——— to indulge me with the possession of her person for one night previous to her departure. We saw from the first, that it would be attended with some difficulty to accomplish this point; but as neither of us was inclined to be disappointed, it was agreed that she should pretend some domestic business at Sheen, which would detain her there all night, a day or two before their departure; and as there was no possibility of our sleeping there, that she should meet me at a place agreed upon, and that we should proceed from thence to some tavern, from whence she might repair to Soho-square, at an early hour the next morning. This scheme was put in execution with the utmost success. We met, drove off to Clapham, indulged ourselves as long as the night would allow, and returned to town by eight o'clock in the morning; at which hour we concluded Mr. D——— would be still a-bed. But our inauspicious stars had otherwise ordained it. The whole matter was discovered. A servant had been sent the night before to Sheen, and had told Mr. D———, upon being asked what time his mistress would be in town, that she had left Sheen early the foregoing day, and had not mentioned any intention of sleeping there.

Mr. D———, alarmed at this intelligence, demanded of his wife as soon as she came home, in a tone of authority, where she had slept. The manner in which he addressed her evinced his suspicions; and she had the presence of mind to declare without the smallest hesitation, that she had slept with Mrs. G———, who was an intimate of the family's. But Mr. D———, still unconvinced, mounted his horse, and set off immediately to that lady, who lived at some distance from town, to prove the truth of her assertion.

As soon as he had left the house, Mrs. D——— came to my lodgings, and told me the circumstances of this unfortunate adventure as I have related them, begging me at the same time to go immediately to Mrs. G———, and entreat her to confirm all that she had said. I instantly complied with her request, and set off in a post-chaise and four; but Mr. D——— had got the start of me, and had taken possession of Mrs. G———'s dressing-room before my arrival. I was therefore reduced to the necessity of writing to her from the inn: but all my persuasion was ineffectual: she had dealt candidly with Mr. D———, and now, as I afterwards learnt, put my note into his hand.

Upon my return to town, Mrs. D——— made up her mind to remain with me, as it was impossible for her to return to Soho-square; and, as I had injured Mr. D——— in so tender a manner, I could not satisfy my own conscience without immediately making him an offer of that reparation which one gentleman has a right to demand of another: but, though I made him the most liberal proposal as a man of honor, he did not condescend to notice my letter on the subject. And I must here observe, in justice to my own character, that I have the satisfaction to say, though my conscience accuses me of all those frailties which are sanctioned by fashion; yet in the very heart of licentiousness, folly, and imprudence, I have preserved my *honor still unsullied*, and can defy the malice of the world to point out a single circumstance in which I ever avoided an appeal to the sword, where personal injury had been sustained!*

But to return: As it might have been attended with some little inconvenience for Mrs. D——— to continue with me in my old lodgings, we removed the same night to an hotel, where we continued for two days; and, on the third, took up our residence

---

* I am sensible that many persons will think this declaration a little erroneous, as I have violated almoſt every moral virtue at some one period or another of my life; and to shew them that I can joke upon this idea as well as themselves, I shall quote a little anecdote of Smollet's, in his Humphry Clinker, which will let this matter in a very pleasant point of view. Speaking of a person that had been pronouncing a panegyric on his friend, and at the the same time ſtigmatizing him with the want of every moral principle – 'This puts me in mind,' says he, 'of a conteſt I once overheard in the way of altercation, betwixt two apple-women in Spring Gardens. One of these viragos having hinted something to the prejudice of the other's moral charaĉter, her antagoniſt, setting her hands in her sides, replied, – 'Speak out, hussey! I scorn your malice – I own I'm both a whore and a thief; and what more have you to say? Damn you, what more have you to say?' 'Bating that, which all the world knows, I challenge you to say, black is the white of my eye.'

in apartments provided for our reception at Somers Town,[37] where we proposed to remain till the affair was in some degree blown over. But we were not long fated to enjoy this repose. On the third morning after our arrival at this place, the house was disturbed at a very early hour by a loud and repeated knocking at the door, and in a few minutes I saw myself surrounded by a gang of bailiffs, and arrested for a hundred and thirty odd pounds, at the suit of Mr. D————. I was immediately hurried away from my little partner in iniquity; she was sent home to her mother, and I saw myself transported from the seat of pleasure, and held in *durance vile* within the magical compass of a spunging-house.[38]

I now, for the first time, began to reflect upon my folly, and curse my imprudence which had brought me into this scene of distress. But as I was doomed to flutter round my cage without a possibility of escaping, I was resolved to make the hours glide by as pleasantly as possible, and immediately dispatched a messenger for Mrs. *New*,[39] and her friend the *conjuror*, who had foretold many scenes of my life, and whom I was determined to consult once more upon the future prospect of my affairs. This scientific gentleman held out but a melancholy prospect to my view, and advised me either to bail or discharge the debt for which I was arrested, and make the best of my way to the continent before Mr. D———— could have time to bring an action of damages against me. But I found this a very difficult matter to accomplish, as in a few days detainers were lodged against me to the amount of four hundred pounds, which it was absolutely necessary to discharge. The only possible means I had of obtaining money, was by offering the clothing of my regiment to some gentleman who might be induced to advance the sum I required; but every man of eminence in London declined the offer. Those who had either wives or daughters, were not willing to oblige a man who might the next day seduce their whole family, and destroy their peace of mind; and those who had money were not willing to lend it to a man devoid of principle, and who had no visible means of repaying it.

I continued in this melancholy situation till the very day appointed for my removal to Newgate; when two very honest gentlemen, a linen-draper and an accoutrement-maker, accepted the clothing of my regiment, went bail for Mr. D———'s debt (the legality of which I thought proper to dispute, though I am actually indebted to him in the sum of *two thousand three hundred pounds** at this moment), and advanced me sufficient sum of ready-money to procure my liberation, and transport me to the continent, where I arrived in the course of a very few days, accompanied by Mrs. D———.

I am now waiting with the utmost solicitude to hear the event of a trial pending in the Court of King's Bench, and which may probably be decided before this publication may meet the eyes of the world. But whatever the determination of the jury in that business may be, I have very little hope of ever being able to return to *England*, without finishing the last days of a miserable existence in all the horrors of confinement.

---

* It may not be improper to mention here, that I gave Mr. D——— a bond in judgment for the two thousand pounds I mentioned as his having lent me to discharge my debts, and a power of attorney to dispose of my eſtate in Ireland, and pay off the mortgages on it, which amounted to eight thousand pounds, besides some years' intereſt upon the whole; but as the bond was not due, and I had revoked the power of attorney upon the discovery of my connexion with Mrs, D———, he was left entirely without any security for his money, which it will moſt certainly never be in my power to pay. But to prevent the possibility of any proceedings againſt my eſtate, I have, by the advice of my attorney, filed a bill in Chancery againſt Mr. D———; which, if it is of no other service, will at leaſt give me time to dispose of every thing I possess, and leave him nothing to claim.

In this country I shall at least have one advantage at the moment I close my eyes on the world; and that is, if I die unpitied, I shall also die unknown; and if I have not the blessings of the multitude as I sink into my grave, I shall at least avoid the curses and imprecations of injured innocence on my head.

POSTSCRIPT

My fate is at length determined. – Since the foregoing pages were committed to the press, I have received the following letter from a friend, which contains the melancholy intelligence of a decree that shuts all ports of *England* against me for ever.

London, Feb. 22, 1792.

My Dear General,
 THE business is over, and I am sorry to tell you that your pastimes with Mrs. D———— are valued at *Five Thousand Pounds.* But do not let this intelligence depress you; we shall move for a new trial, place every thing in *statu quo,* and if we can but collect a few weather-beaten scrubs of iniquity to compose the jury, we may still bring you off for *Five Shillings.*

 You have very great friends in court, I assure you, and we have every thing to hope from a second trial. Your character is now pretty well known; every body execrates you, and your infamy is the common topic of discourse; you have, therefore, *nothing* to lose on the score of reputation; and a man may easily compound for a little temporary scandal, when *Four Thousand Nine Hundred and Ninety-nine Pounds Fifteen Shillings* is the possible recompense.

 Your hints with respect to D———— and Mrs. G————,[40] received some inimitable sets-off, and were represented to the life. The story was well put together on *your* part; but, between ourselves, it was a most infamous and diabolical scheme of retaliation; but, *mum!* for that – I am as silent as the grave – though I hope in God the Colonel may not meet you on the Continent.

I am told he is a damned impetuous mercurial kind of a fellow; and should he take the law into his hands, the Lord have mercy on your *honor's* bones!

Your old friend *Betty H————*[41] swore like an angel, and rolled you on the carpet with admirable dexterity. The game of *blind-man's-buff*[42] went off with infinite *eclat;* and though *Erskine*[43] mauled you most divinely, I really believe we should have come off with flying colours, in spite of the crusty old puts who composed the jury, had it not been for that damned *sacred deposit.* – Why 'twas like taking the earnest of your ruin! – Ah! General, General! no other man would ever have split upon that rock; but you *men of honor,* forsooth, can never, as you yourself say, *even in the most desperate situations,* deviate from the *punctilio* which is the rule of your conduct.

Remember me to your *dear little seducer,* and let her know that we shall delay her affair in the Commons as long as possible, for a certain reason. *A-propos,* I beg I may be looked upon as the sponsor of the sweet embryo that is coming. I claim the preference in this particular upon a relationship in *principle.* – As it will be the *child of iniquity,* where can you find so proper a god-father for it as an *attorney?*

I remain,

My dear General,

Yours, &c.

General G————.

P. S. Do you think either your *agent* or *clothier* will stretch as far as five hundred more ? – Perhaps you may persuade them to make it up between-them. – We have very empty pockets at present; and you know, my dear General, the war cannot be carried on without money.

P. S. It is whispered here, that you have resolved in a fit of compunction to publish your life; but it is surely nothing more than report. For Heaven's sake, my dear General, mind what you are about – I fear you are ill-advised – at any rate do not mention a word of * If you touch upon that, a new trial is a joke, and we are all blown up at once.

Thus the storm is past, and with it are departed the poor re-mains of that honor which once adorned my name. In vain the most artful schemes were formed, in vain the most seducing eloquence displayed, to soften the austerity of those virtues that sat in judgment upon me. Neither the infatuating splendor of the one, nor the persuasive villany of the other, joined to the favorable representations of a *merciful* judge, could avert my fate, and turn the bolt of Heaven from its destined object. – I have received the blow, and the wound is sunk too deep, I fear, ever to be healed.

What if I yield to the persuasion of my advocate, and submit my case once more to the compassion of a jury; have I any thing to hope from a tribunal, at which, I have been already judged, but additional disgrace, and accumulated ruin? Am I not suffi-ciently stigmatized? Will these pretended friends tear the mask from my face, and leave me no covering for features marked with infamy and vice? I would they would cease to goad me:

> They prune a rotten tree,
> That cannot so much as a blossom yield.

And yet their persecutions know no end.

My mind is the seat of phrensy and distraction. I dare not look forward, for that would be to anticipate a series of evils which are still preserved to mark the latter period of my days; and to look back, is to behold a train of bitter reflections rising, as it were, in judgment against me. The present moment, discoloured as it is, is all I dare survey; and in it I behold the sad *memento* of my former vices and my future punishment. *Oh! that I were,* as Job said, in the piety of his heart, *as in months past: when I washed my steps with butter, and caused the widow's heart to sing with gladness!* But now the golden, scenes, the years of splendor that my faithless fortune promised from my earliest days, are gone for ever ; and I may exclaim with the haughty Wolsey, in the hour of his degradation:

Vain pomp and grandeur of the worlds I hate you!

THE END.

APPENDIX

AFFIDAVIT SWORN BY ELIZABETH GUNNING, 14 FEBRUARY 1791

Accusations alledged against me.

1. I am accused of having written letters in the name of the Duke of Marlborough and of Lord Blandford, and also of writing anonymous letters.

2. I am accused of going to Mrs. Bowen's lodgings, on Sunday, the 6th of February, about the forged letters produced by her.

3. I am accused of having bribed papa's groom, not to go to Blenheim with a letter from papa to the Duke of Marlborough, and a a narrative of my writing which I had drawn out at the request of papa for the purpose (as he said) of being sent to the Duke and Duchess of Marlborough; that I bribed the groom not *really* to go to Blenheim, but to *say* he had been there, and to deliver, as coming from the Duke of Marlborough, a letter that I had given him for that purpose.

My answers on Oath.

1. I never have written, nor caused to be written any letter, or note, in my whole life, in a disguised hand, by a fictitious name or anonymous.

2. I never was in Mrs. Bowen's lodgings in my life; I never met her by appointment, or by chance, at any third place: the only place I have ever seen her, has been at my father's house, or in my father's carriage, and never without my mama or my aunt being present. I never wrote her a note or a letter in my life; I never spoke to her confidentially on any subject whatever.

3. I never spoke to papa's groom, or caused him to be spoken to, prior to, or on the subject of, his journey to Blenheim, and that the letter he brought back was from the Duke of Marlborough; and I felt happy and grateful for the honour his Grace had done me.

NOTES

1. A snake lies in the grass.
2. When Elizabeth and Maria Gunning attended a ball at Dublin Castle in 1748, Thomas Sheridan furnished the impoverished girls with costumes for Juliet and Lady Macbeth from th theatre's costume department. His son was the famous Richard Brinsley Sheridan.
3. Lord Chesterfield's *Letters to His Son* (1774). On the whole, these have a high moral tone. It is hard to see why Gunning should regard them as any part of his education in debauchery.
4. Clarissa Harlowe, the tragic heroine of Samuel Richardson's *Clarissa, or, the History of a Young Lady* (1748). Although there is a lot of sex in this novel, the heroine is the innocent victim of unscrupulous men.
5. Presumably vixen, although Clarissa is a virtuous woman.
6. Loveless, i.e. Robert Lovelace, the villain who rapes Clarissa.
7. See above.
8. The Romans and Greeks used to place a piece of cake in the hands of the dead, to mollify Cerberus, the three-headed hound which guarded the underworld.
9. Lawrence Sterne, *A Sentimental Journey through France and Italy* (1768).
10. Echoing, of course, the title of Goldsmith's play, *She Stoops to Conquer* (1773).
11. William Shenstone (1714–1763), poet and gardener.
12. Head to foot.
13. Barbara of Cilli, wife of the Holy Roman Emperor, Sigsmund. She was called the 'Messalina of Germany', although, unlike Messalina, there is no indication that she was a nymphomaniac.
14. Actually, there are 144.
15. Apparently a reference to the radical, Thomas Paine who published *The Rights of Man* (referred to in the footnote)in 1791. Paine was born in 1737 and was therefore older than the General. This is the strongest indication (other than the outrageous nature of the whole

work) that the *Apology* may be a hoax. The footnote also mentions common sense. Paine published a pamphlet in 1776 with that title, arguing against British rule in America.

16.   This time the author has understated the number. It should be 135.

17.   A *petit maître* is an effeminate man, a fop.

18.   Another quotation from Sterne, *A Sentimental Journey through France and Italy.*

19.   Abélard was castrated by Héloïse's uncle, canon Fulbert.

20.   And yet, Gunning was no more than fifty-two in 1792.

21.   This occurs in *Letters Writ by a Turkish Spy* by Giovanni Paolo Marana, first published between 1684 and 1686. The first English edition appeared in 1687.

22.   A *put* is a blockhead.

23.   Criminal conversation, adultery.

24.   Both myrtle and rose were sacred to Aphrodite, the goddess of love.

25.   Bernard de Fontenelle, *Lettres Galantes du Chevalier d'Her* (1685): [I'll search out] graces that laugh and loves that frolic.

26.   In this context, a coif is a white cap formerly worn by lawyers, particularly serjeants-at-law.

27.   In the twenty-ninth year of the reign of Charles II. Although Charles wasn't crowned until 1661, legal documents were dated as though he had succeeded to the throne on his father's death in 1649, so the date referred to is 1678. The author is clearly recycling a very old story.

28.   Adam was said to have lived 930 years, Methuselah 962. Many other antediluvians were remarkable for their longevity.

29.   Another example of Gunning (or someone writing as him) recycling very old material. This story appeared in the *Spectator* on 13 June 1711.

30.   Lorne.

31.   Argyll.

32.   Blandford.

33.   Bowen.

34.   '… Yet (by your gracious patience) | I will a round unvarnish'd tale deliver…' Othello, I. iii. 89–90.

35.   General Gunning was appointed Colonel of the 65th Regiment of Foot in 1788.

36.   James Duberley.

37. At the time the *Apology* was written, a relatively new North London suburb.
38. A public house used by the authorities as a temporary place of confinement for debtors.
39. I have been unable to identify the fortune-telling Mrs New.
40. There was no suggestion during the trial that Duberley had an affair with Mrs Gunning but he was said to keep a mistress.
41. Betty H_____, one of the defence witnesses, Elizabeth Hurst.
42. Gunning's defence counsel claimed that the Duberleys played blind man's buff in company, a recreation which he suggested was quite improper (although it can hardly be considered a solitary occupation).
43. Counsel for the plaintiff.

INDEX

TIGER OF THE STRIPE

TYPESET IN THE UNITED KINGDOM
BY TIGER OF THE STRIPE
IN ADOBE CASLON PRO USING
ADOBE INDESIGN CS6

ALSO FROM TIGER OF THE STRIPE

Conversations on the
Plurality of Worlds

BERNARD DE FONTENELLE

Translated by Elizabeth Gunning

Buy from Amazon:

Amazon US

Amazon UK

Kindle

http://www.pluralityofworlds.com